©Roxanna Walitzki

ABOUT THE AUTHOR
Siolo Thompson

———◆———

Siolo Thompson is a writer and illustrator based in the Pacific Northwest. She is known for her narrative illustration style and delicate watercolor renderings of the natural world. She holds a BA in Comparative Literature and an MFA in Creative Writing. Her work, published by Llewellyn, can be seen in the Linestrider Tarot, the Hedgewitch Oracle, and the Otherkin Tarot.

MEETING THE
Otherkin

MEETING THE
Otherkin

Siolo Thompson

Llewellyn Worldwide, Woodbury, Minnesota

First Edition
First Printing

Book design by Cassie Willett
Cover design by Shira Atakpu
Cover art and card illustrations © 2019 by Siolo Thompson
Llewellyn Publications is a registered trademark of Llewellyn Worldwide Ltd.

ISBN: 978-0-7387-5873-2

The Otherkin Tarot kit consists of a boxed set of 78 full-color cards and this perfect bound book.

Llewellyn Publications
A Division of Llewellyn Worldwide Ltd.
2143 Wooddale Drive
Woodbury, MN 55125-2989
www.llewellyn.com

Printed in China

This book and tarot deck are dedicated to Jordan Mooney.
May you shine bright among the stars forever.

CONTENTS

CHAPTER 3

◆

INTRODUCTION

Welcome to the Otherkin Tarot. Here you will find a world that is both strange and familiar—both *other* and *kin*. Each of the seventy-eight cards in this unique deck feature a being who inhabits the liminal space between myth and fact, human and animal. A lion with the body of a man sits on the Emperor's throne; selkies cavort with mermaids; frogs and foxes take on human garb; and a sagacious owl acts as Hierophant. The deep symbolism of the tarot is brought into new light with these fanciful illustrations that address the underlying archetypes of traditional decks. Most closely following the Rider-Waite-Smith system, Otherkin is an easy entry to tarot for beginners and for the more experienced it reads with gentle humor and a trickster edge. One of the distinguishing features of the Otherkin deck is the attention given not just to the major arcana but to each of the pips as well. Every card in the deck features a character or characters that bring the themes to life, from the High Priestess to the Two of Pentacles.

The artwork of Otherkin was created with hand-ground organic pigments on unbleached, hand-made paper. The resulting effect is lovely and muted, boasting none of the pristine whites or vibrant primary colors of other decks. Here is a deck that welcomes wear and tear, a deck that wants to travel and be left out in the moonlight. It is not precious. It will improve with every use. My hope is that this will be a "go to" deck for the querent rather than a collector's item that forever sits on the sidelines gathering dust.

Accompanying this deck is a full-length text that explores not just the traditional meaning of each of the cards but their archetypal underpinnings. Additionally, the text speaks of associations—plants and planets, animals and art. Like the Linestrider before it, the Otherkin Tarot was a labor of love that was created with deep personal investment in both the text and artwork.

"Otherkin" is a word sometimes employed by folks who strongly identify with a nonhuman counterpart. This identification may feel like a particular affinity for an animal such as a wolf or fox or perhaps something deeper or more ancestral. In creating the Otherkin deck, I tried to tap into the energies of these archetypes to find their kin in the animal realm and among the mythic figures that occupy hallowed places in our legends and lore. Some of the tarot cards manifested easily others took longer for me to understand but in the end this deck is filled with a cast of characters that I hope will be both familiar and invigorating.

There are so many wonderful tarot decks in the world, and the Otherkin deck may be just one among a large collection or the very first deck you have owned. Every practitioner has their own customs and quirks when it comes to handling and using the decks, and we all find ours over time, which is one of the delights of tarot. Specific decks often seem to present their own challenges and peculiarities. Some decks speak most clearly about interpersonal communication and relationships while others only want to talk about action and ambition.

There is no substitute for time and use when it comes to understanding a particular deck. You may immediately bond to a deck or you may have thought a deck was going to be perfect for you only to find that as much as you like the art, you just can't get a clear reading from it. As a tarot collector myself, I sometimes struggle to enter into conversation with a new set. Sometimes it is just a matter of familiarity and time; like a friendship, connection may happen slowly. Making up my own spreads or doing random pulls can also help me bond more easily. While it seems scary to write on a deck, I also believe adding things to the cards can make them more yours—I've found that embellishing, adding borders, or taking notes directly on the cards can speed up the dialog. I saw an example of this when I met Heru Jerome, a tarot reader in Brooklyn who gave me a reading; he had notes, sigils, and symbols written directly on the card faces! He had a very seamless facility with his deck, and you could see a deep understanding present between him and the cards. Another really simple thing to try with new decks is to carry them around, close to your body, for a few weeks. Slip a new deck into your purse or put it under your pillow.

At the end of the day, tarot is a practice based in intuition. Each of us must develop our own methods and traditions for tarrying with the tarot. Have fun, try not to force things, practice deep listening. My sincere hope is that this deck and your tarot practice in general will enrich your experience in the world and aid you in your journey. In the next section you will find some basic layouts and reading methods. There are many other ways to read the cards—this is by no means an exhaustive guide—but I do hope that some of this information will be useful.

Cheers and happy reading!

CHAPTER 1

———◆———

READING
THE CARDS

The illustrations featured on the Otherkin tarot deck endeavor to provide clear information and visual clues that will help a querent navigate the system of meaning. If you are familiar with the Rider-Waite-Smith deck, you should have no trouble with the Otherkin system with a little practice. Each card nods to the RWS deck while hopefully bringing its unique whimsy and message to a reading. For example, the juggling man on the RWS Two of Pentacles becomes a lemur perched on a tree branch with golden eyes and perfect balance. The Empress in the Otherkin deck is a woman with the head of a bear, reminding us of the fierceness of maternal instinct and the power of a woman in full.

There are as many tarot reading traditions as there are tarot card readers, and that is as it should be. Our unique and individual approach to reading is what makes it such a fun and rewarding practice. While the core associations and deep archetypes remain present in each card, our own perspectives on life will affect our ways of reading.

USING SIGNIFIERS

A signifier card, sometimes called a significator, is a single card selected from the tarot deck that represents the querent in their present state or the specific aspirations the querent may have. This card is used to center a reading and request specific information. Many people find themselves drawn to a single card in which they see a representation of themselves. For example, a teacher may choose the Hierophant, or an artist might immediately gravitate toward the Queen of Cups. Placing this card in a central position in a reading can help the querent connect more strongly to the deck. If there is a specific energy or goal you have in mind, a significator can be used for that purpose as well.

EXALTATION OF ACES

Exalting an ace is a practice that treats the aces as overall themes or mood signifiers. If you pull cards for a layout and discover an ace on reveal, move it to the side and pull a new card to replace the ace. Now, note the way in which the reading is "flavored" by the ace. An Ace of Pentacles will steer the reading toward the physical, material, or financial. The Ace of Swords will speak of the mind, clarity, and the realm of ideas. An Ace of Wands addresses action, creativity, and movement. The Ace of Cups will turn our attention to relationships, intuition, and spirituality. The specificity of this may help you be more prepared and able to deal with emerging challenges.

TOWER TRUMPS ALL

The Tower is a powerful card, arguably the strongest in the deck. Some readers believe that the Tower always exists in present tense and that regardless of where it shows up in a reading, the querent should prepare for implications in their current situation. If the Tower manifests in the past position, indicating a major life change in the past (for example, the loss of a loved one or an early success that altered your path), that Tower moment will always be with you, even though it is behind you now. Every aspect of your life has been affected by the Tower's major change or upheaval.

When you see a Tower in the future position, you can be certain that big changes are underway, like a tidal wave that is miles out to sea but gradually rolling toward shore. Be it past, present, or future, you can seldom avoid the effects of this card but can generally rely on the cards around the Tower to offer clues about the aspects of your life most affected by this kind of big life event. Pentacles may indicate that the fallout is financial, while cups indicate relationships that are at risk. There are many ways you can prepare for the Tower if you see it coming, and there are ways to deal with the damage from past Tower events.

REVERSED READING

Many choose to read reversed cards, and reversed meanings for each card are given in this book. This deck is designed with reversed readings in mind, for that reason the card back is identical top to bottom.

In general, tarot cards are not meant to be read individually. There are exceptions, of course—you can do a one-card draw or a yes/no reading—but each tarot card has intricate layers of meaning that often depend on the other cards to tell the story of a situation and guide the querent toward the best path. They form a puzzle, an interlocking and multilayered lasagna of guidance. There are nuances to reversals that can be helpful, and I included them because I believe they bring additional insight to a reading…but they are certainly not required.

In fact, reversals are entirely optional; when the deck really wants to warn you about something, you don't need to see the card upside-down to understand what's up. For example, the combination of Temperance, the Knight of Cups, and the Devil in any orientation tells you that you can be pretty sure that the sexy bartender you met on Tuesday has a drinking problem!

THROWING THE CARDS

If you are new to tarot, here are a few card layouts to help you get started. You might like to use different spreads for each question, situation, or person you are reading for. If a querent is struggling to choose between two options, you can use a card arrangement that compares and contrasts rather than something that speaks more simply of one issue. Many of you are seasoned tarot readers and already have set layouts. Whether you are an old hand at tarot or new to the cards, you should always listen to your intuition rather than adhere to tradition or the mandates of others. Your relationship with tarot is unique and will go its own direction, but here are a few of my favorite spreads to get you started.

THREE-CARD SPREAD

The three-card spread is a quick and easy layout that most directly addresses a particular question or situation. Most commonly the cards are read as past–present–future. Three cards may not be enough information to really get a full picture, especially when the information you seek is about relationships which can be incredibly nuanced and complex.

When using a three-card spread, don't feel as though past–present–future is the only approach; you can let your intuition guide you toward other interpretations. For example, if you are thinking about a specific problem or course of action you may frame your query as problem–cause–solution. Or, you can think about the problem in the framework of time: What can I do right now? What can I do in the short term? What potential does this situation have in the long term? No matter how it is used, this layout provides a snapshot of influencing elements or potential outcomes. It can be quite useful when you are doing readings at an event or in a social situation as you can get a quick picture without delving too deeply into things.

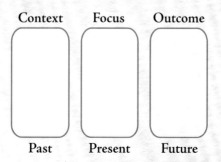

FIVE-CARD SPREAD

This is an easy layout that focuses on a primary question or situation and brings influencing elements into the reading. It's a little more fleshed out than the three-card draw but is still easy to track. There are a number of ways you can arrange the cards, though I generally favor putting a card for the present or even a significator card in the central position and setting the cards up in the shape of a cross. Above the central card is the card representing the potential or the potential outcome. To the left of you are past influences, and to the right are future elements or where the situation is heading. The bottom card is what I call "the question," but it can also be seen as the card that helps you examine your motivations.

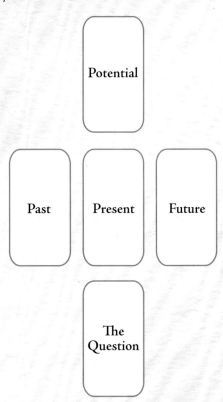

CHAPTER 2

—◆—

MAJOR ARCANA

THE FOOL

Keywords: Idealism, adventures, innocence, decisions, spontaneity, risk taking, naivety, open mindedness

The Fool is a card of new beginnings, enthusiasm, and innocence. As the card that represents zero, or the starting point in tarot, it is pure potential. On this card we see a figure happily skipping along, ready to step off into the unknown. The Fool shows no fear—he is full of joy and accept the world, come what may. The card embodies the leap of faith that allows you to move forward even when you don't know what is going to happen or what lies ahead. Here is the beginning of your journey, when you are still fresh and unburdened by the weight of life. As you learn tarot, you'll notice that it teaches everything is a cycle, so this card can also represent where you can hope to end up—a state of perfect acceptance where you can be joyful, adventurous, and open to the beauty of the world. In readings, the Fool often foretells a new beginning, change of direction, or new path that will lead to personal growth. If you are seeing this card in a moment of decision, the Fool reminds you to trust your instincts and choose the things in life that truly speak to your soul.

In a work, business, or professional reading, the Fool represents the fearless entrepreneurial spirit that charges ahead despite not quite knowing how things might turn out. The Fool figure is often pictured as a beggar or wanderer with tattered clothes and a patched tunic. Despite knowing what it is to have nothing, the Fool is fearless—he does not cling to the past or ideas about the future. Every day is an adventure and must be lived on its own terms. This card instructs you to not hold your resources too tightly. You have to risk something if you are going to gain anything. There is a youthful and joyous energy associated with the Fool. When you see this card in a relationship, love, or friendship reading, it generally advises you to accept adventure, keep an open mind, and try something new. If you get caught up in your ideas about the perfect situation or your fear of betrayal, you will close the door on possibilities and opportunities for growth. There is an element of naiveté here that the Fool would rather accept than examine. You may be avoiding a difficult truth or feel unwilling to let go of something that is not as idyllic as you thought it would be.

In reverse, this card cautions you against enthusiasm without proof and faith without evidence. The Fool is beautiful because of the open, willing, accepting energy he represents, but often the world will take that energy and turn it back on itself. Be alive and open to the world, but don't be so trusting that negative forces can reach you. You can be enthusiastic with care and skeptical without cynicism.

------- ◆ -------

THE MAGICIAN

*Keywords: power, focus, goal attainment,
study, communication, transformation, magic*

One of the most powerful and magical cards in the deck, the Magician has dominion over all of the elements. She is depicted here as a female figure with antlers, but the Magician transcends gender and corporeal form, a being of power and connection and glamour. Most strongly associated with consciousness and creativity in action this is a goal attainment and connectivity card related to the Mercurius of alchemy and to the number one. A true card of powerful beginnings, this is one of the best omens you can see at the start of a new venture or relationship. The eternity symbol generally present in any depiction of this card indicates a connection with the eternal and with things outside the physical realm.

How can you channel the power of the universe toward your goals? This is the question the Magician seeks to answer. In a professional, work, or financial reading, the Magician is a good omen when you are dealing with creative projects or seeking advancement in a particular area. There are times in life when everything seems to be on your side, and that is when the Magician is in your house and you are allowing that power to flow. This is especially true when paired with the Fool; joy, an openness to intuition, natural charisma—these are just some of the Magician's aspects. In love, friendship, and relationship readings, this energy can be a great gift as it allows you to bring others in and be open to the gifts they offer while still holding your own place and power.

Reversed, you can be sure this card is indicating an area in your life that is holding you back from your full potential. Does your creative energy feel blocked, your enthusiasm dampened, or your relationships stagnant? The Magician reversed can give strong indications about what changes need to be made so that you can move forward toward your best self.

————◆————

THE HIGH PRIESTESS

Keywords: intuition, the subconscious, magic,
feeling, rituals, dreams, symbols

The High Priestess and the Hierophant stand on opposite shores. The Hierophant urges emphasis on the intellect and organizations, while the High Priestess wants you to trust your subconscious and celebrate your individuality. She is intensely connected to the feminine divine and stands at the division between the conscious and unconscious realms. Almost always depicted with pomegranates to symbolize Persephone and her yearly sojourn into the underworld, this card reminds you that there is more to life than the things you can see and control; look beyond the surface, trust your intuition, read the signs. In the Otherkin tarot deck, the High Priestess is pictured as a beautiful water creature embracing a lobster. The lobster, who you will encounter again in the Moon card, is an emissary of the subconscious realm and a symbol of intuition, dreams, and spirituality.

In a work or financial reading, the High Priestess represents a move toward creativity, intuition, and the feminine. In a romance or relationship reading, the High Priestess urges you to trust your subconscious. Do you have anxiety or doubts about someone? Trust your intuition: if your gut tells you there is a problem, don't let anyone else convince you otherwise. This dynamic is especially true if you see swords in your reading—a Two of Swords, for example, speaks to not having all the facts and encourages more research to see clearly. A High Priestess may signify that someone new is entering your life— this person will have a strong feminine energy and likely will be an emotional and spiritual person.

The High Priestess reversed cautions against ignoring your intuition or inner voice. If you are being overly influenced by others or are following a path based too much in the physical realm, you may see this as cautionary. The High Priestess often tells the querent to seek solitude, self-motivated study, and personal development, especially when paired with the Hermit. If your voice is being overwhelmed by others, you need to take the time and space to reconnect with your own intuition and desires. In reverse this card can also caution against paranoia. She urges us to trust our intuition, yes, but at the same time it is also good to remember that others are seldom working directly against us. In the case of hidden agendas or the machinations of others, look for conflict cards in your reading.

———◆———

THE EMPRESS

Keywords: matriarchy, power, strength, fertility, creativity, passion, abundance, children, motherhood, prosperity

The Empress is the ultimate feminine archetype, pictured in this deck as half human, half bear—an animal often associated with the fierceness of a mother protecting her cubs. She is power and sexuality ruled by Venus; the Empress is both huntress and homemaker. Her crown of stars reminds us that this is a fully developed individual connected to the cosmos. She is the feminine divine risen to power, a ruler, matriarch, and leader. Her nudity is a celebration of the female body that gives life, comfort, and strength.

In a business or financial reading, the Empress represents prosperity, fertility, and abundance, and she is an excellent omen for those who are beginning new ventures or projects. This card is an indication that the seeds you are sowing will grow but must be mothered into their full potential. If you are in a position of leadership, you may be called upon to act with compassion to nurture, mentor, or advocate for someone. There are many ways to show authority and garner the respect of others, but kindness and generosity are sometimes the traits that most effectively encourage loyalty and bring out the best in others. The Empress in a relationship reading can indicate a strong connection to the feminine or a need for one. She is a good omen for fertility and reproduction and can also speak to deepening the connection with existing family, especially children. Here is a powerful woman who embodies the best qualities of a matriarch, representing either the energy the querent should welcome into their life or a specific person—the querent, a love interest, a strong female figure—who is influencing the situation. As a symbol of fertility and motherhood, the Empress is a great card to see at the beginning of a new relationship as she indicates that there is potential in the situation for growth and power.

Reversed, the Empress can indicate that your energy is being drained by something or that you are not recharging in a way that allows you to fulfill your maximum potential. Are you spending so much time mothering others (children, employees, projects) to the point where you have no energy left to grow and prosper? People who have the kind of potential this card represents are very attractive to others, and their energy, time, and affection are always in demand. If you are this person, a queen or king among the common rabble, you must develop strategies to protect your time and energy. The Empress reversed can also speak to possessiveness and jealousy in yourself or those around you. If you are struggling with fertility, pregnancy, or getting a nascent idea or project into a growth phase, you may also see this lady reversed.

———————◆———————

THE EMPEROR

Keywords: power, leadership, authority,
maturity, stubbornness, judgment, masculinity

The Emperor is the ultimate patriarchal figure in the tarot deck. He is regal, powerful, and unyielding. The Emperor is usually depicted as a rigid character upon a throne, upright, bedecked in regal robes, holding some kind of scepter—a fairly phallic reminder of his masculine power. He often sports a white beard and hair, which speak to his age and the wisdom and authority that come with experience. The color red and the element fire are often present in depictions of the Emperor, a reminder of both the power of this king and his capacity for anger. The strong patriarchal energy of this card may not be welcomed by every querent, but the Emperor represents more than just a domineering father figure. He can bring a message of empowerment, leadership, and authority or may also indicate an ally who exhibits these characteristics.

In a work reading, the Emperor indicates authority, discipline, and structure. Has the time come for you to move into a role that carries more responsibility? The Emperor is not shy about wearing that crown or waving his … umm, scepter around. He announces his authority with authority. Depending on the placement in a spread and the querent's state of mind, this card may also speak of someone in your professional life. In a relationship reading, an older man or patriarchal figure may be a potential mate for you or you may be in the position of assuming a patriarchal role in someone's life. In a general relationship reading or family reading, the Emperor can simply indicate the head of household or patriarch.

In reverse this card can have strong negative connotations and may caution against anger, abuse of power, and a destructive authoritarian attitude. While rule of law brings order to the land, those same mechanisms can be devastating when wielded without compassion. If this card is addressing you directly, it's time to examine the way you are operating in the world. This could be an indication that current difficulties are a direct result of your own controlling or inflexible behavior. Let's not forget that most of the time, Zeus was an out-of-control warmonger with a penchant for rape.

———◆———

THE HIEROPHANT

Keywords: organizations, hierarchy, community, study,
corporations, rituals, religious affiliations, conventionality, traditions

The Otherkin Hierophant card greets us with a sagacious owl who represents tradition, hierarchy, and institutions and their values. This card often urges the querent to pursue a course of formal study, seek membership in an organization, or participate more fully in a corporation or structured work environment. While a card like the Hermit suggests solitude and self-motivated study, the Hierophant almost always speaks of self-improvement via organizations and institutions. This card can also represent a person who follows rules or is most comfortable within a highly structured environment. Like his counterpart, the High Priestess, the Hierophant guards the doors to secret realms. The High Priestess is a scion of the subconscious, feeling, intuition, and dreams, while the Hierophant stands for the opposite—the intellect, worldly knowledge, formal structures. The number three is represented in the Otherkin deck by the three symbols on the owl's body and by the three fingers of the benediction hand. The Hierophant in its ultimate form unites the three realms of mental, physical, and spiritual. Here is the wise leader, priest, or head of an organization who has the potential to become guru-like when developing the full range of their powers. Notice the stack of books upon which the Hierophant is perched—it is both an indication of the things the Hierophant represents and also the key to his own power. The Hierophant is knowledgeable, learned, and an authority in his field.

In a work, professional, or financial reading, the Hierophant usually indicates a deeper involvement with an institution or company. For example, you may see the Hierophant if you are considering going back to school, joining a board of directors, or applying for a position within a company. In a romance or relationship reading, the Hierophant can represent a person who is driven by the intellect, rules, or fixed ideas. This person may be a teacher or in law enforcement or the military, or they could simply be a member of an organization that has a strong structure and hierarchy. The Hierophant may also be suggesting that you will find love within an organization, with a classmate, supervisor, instructor, or that bike cop that helped you with your groceries. If your inquiry is about an existing relationship, the indication may be that you need to focus on the mind rather than the heart in this situation.

The Hierophant reversed can represent the negative aspects of formal structures and a need to question leadership or authority. This card may appear when it is time for you to part ways with an institution or Hierophant type. If intellect and adherence to the rules have been driving your momentum, it may be time to shift toward the heart and intuition. The rigidity of the Hierophant can be a tool for success but can also prevent you from seeing and seizing opportunities that require flexibility and an open mind. Remember to balance mind with heart and judgment with intuition.

THE LOVERS

Keywords: partnership, friendship, attraction,
unification, communication, contracts

The Lovers card embodies ideal partnerships, deep communication, and the significant bonds we form with others. Many people interpret this card as romantic (and it certainly has that aspect), but it is also emblematic of other kinds of relationships in which there is a high degree of mutual respect, trust, and commitment. These are the bonds and commitments that enable our progress and help us reach our goals. The Lovers pictured here are holding an egg, a symbol of new life, new ideas, and the fruit that these deep, sincere relationships tend to produce. When we are fully committed to a partnership, we are channeling the energy of the Lovers; that kind of commitment can be a powerful tool in our personal journey.

In business, work, and financial readings, this card urges us to find our place, not just within a business or industry, but within a system that is profoundly aligned to our own values and beliefs. Whether you love animals, state parks, or speculative fiction, let your passion be your guide. This card can also indicate strong professional partnerships. The Lovers is most strongly associated with romantic love, sex, and marriage. In relationship readings you may see this card in the future position, indicating a coming soul mate connection. In the present or influencing positions, this card often means that you already have a deep bond and that it is a source of power and stability that will enable your journey. Beware of conflict cards or cards that indicate deception; this reading may be warning you of the ways in which your relationship is potentially being jeopardized by unresolved issues, careless behaviors, or the actions of others. In a past position, the Lovers can represent a strong example of a relationship—a parental bond, important friendship, or even a past marriage that is a fundamental part of who you are.

In reverse the Lovers warns you about relationships, contracts, or commitments that are in jeopardy. There may be inner conflicts, disharmony, or cowardice that is preventing you from truly committing to things. This card can also most literally represent negative bonds such as relationships that have turned sour, resentment between partners, dishonesty, or a lack of mutual attraction. This card often pops up in readings for people in sexless marriages or long-term relationships. While sex isn't everything, it might be time for you to ask the hard questions. Why has your relationship arrived at this point? What is holding you back? Is it time to move on? Be brutally honest and clear with yourself; you may have some difficult decisions to make.

◆

THE CHARIOT

Keywords: ambition, self-discipline,
goal attainment, sacrifice, movement, victory

Sit up straight and get ready, everyone, because here is one of the tarot deck's power cards! This is a card that speaks strongly of goal attainment, self-actualization, and our ability to rein in our personal drama and take control of our lives. Most depictions of this card involve two beasts, light and dark (horses, sphinxes, or fish, in this case), that represent the opposing forces in your life. The job of the charioteer is to exert her will upon these disparate elements and to bring them not just under control, but to direct these forces towards a greater goal.

The Chariot most frequently appears in professional/financial related readings. This is because job and money endeavors involve imposing your will on the external world, as opposed to relationship readings where the work is more about aligning your will and desires to a partner, friend, or family. The Chariot is a self-centric card. It speaks to your trajectory, the effect you have in the world, and the ways in which you are molding (or seeking to mold) life to fit your specific wants, needs, and desires.

When the Chariot shows up in a relationship or love reading, it often means that either the querent themselves or a significant other is heavily focused on career or financial goals, perhaps to the detriment of other parts of their lives. It can frequently be an admonishment that urges the querent to understand that if all your strength is marshaled toward the attainment of financial or professional goals, you may not have anything left to give the people in your life. If your query is about a potential relationship or someone new entering your life, this card can indicate that your love interest is heavily invested in their own goals and that you should be prepared for a situation in which you or a relationship are not their primary interest. On the flip side, in a love reading this card may indicate that now is a time for you to focus on your own goals rather than becoming overly invested in a relationship.

In reverse the Chariot counsels balance, temperance, and self-care. Sometimes the price of ambition is alienation, loneliness, and ill health. Be aware of those around you and remember that life is more than just making money or getting ahead. The negative aspect of this card addresses the problems that often come with being a workaholic or letting greed or hunger for power negatively affect your life.

◆

STRENGTH

*Keywords: courage, patience, self control,
balance, motivation, inner strength, success*

Strength is a special card that reminds us of what true power is. This card represents a high level of self-mastery, inner strength, and spiritual knowledge. These are not qualities you have by chance; they come from doing the difficult work of understanding and accepting your strengths and weakness. The illustration on this card typically involves a white-robed feminine figure subduing a lion. The lion is clearly the "stronger" of the two, but the woman is able to control him easily. Otherkin's whimsical retelling of this has the white-robed figure replaced by a goose who loosely holds the reins to the lion and steers him toward her objective. The lesson these images hold is that we can control the world not by force but by will, marshaling our own power and internal resources. Properly aligned, the human spirit can overcome any obstacle.

The appearance of the Strength card in business, work, or financial readings can indicate a time when you will be tested. You may be moving into a leadership role, a difficult team, or a stressful shift that will require all your internal resources. In team and leadership scenarios, the Strength card speaks clearly of inspiring respect and loyalty in others not through force or fear but through compassion, mutual respect, and power over your own impulses and reactions. Strength in a relationship, love, or friendship reading often speaks to the kind of internal work we must do in order to offer our best selves to others. This card represents a higher level of consciousness and the kind of honesty that is not about seeing others but rather focuses on taking responsibility for yourself, your past, your actions, and your desires. Seek balance and harmony within yourself before looking outward—*that* is where your power will stem from.

In reverse the Strength card speaks of weakness, self-doubt, and a lack of confidence. Old wounds, harsh words, or criticism may have become internalized in a way that is preventing you from owning your power. You may have suffered an injury or illness that is holding you back. No matter what obstacle you are facing, you can find strength and freedom, but that often means doing the difficult work of radical honesty. Identify the things that are preventing you from maximizing your life and opportunities, and commit to working on them.

———◆———

THE HERMIT

Keywords: study, soul searching, solitude, patience,
withdrawal, reluctant leadership

The Hermit tarot card is most strongly associated with solitude, study, periods of intense self-development, introspection, and inward focus. The Hermit is a scholar, a wise and mature individual who is often sought out for advice or counsel. I am reminded of the hedge witches; healers and shamans who were pushed out of cities and lived beyond the wall or literally beyond the hedge that marked the borders of a town. In many cases they became the only place where the disenfranchised—women, people of color, or queer folk—could find help with injury or illness. The Hermit, with his lantern shining in the dark, is often a reluctant leader. While they would rather just be left alone with their books, they have all the qualities people seek in leadership.

In business, work, or financial readings the Hermit most frequently represents the querent themselves. This card often shows up for us when we need to work on the foundations of our lives. That may mean expanding our skill set, traveling, or embarking on a course of study or certification. The Hermit in love, relationship, and friendship readings indicates that you have become overly influenced by others or that your internal voice is being drowned out by someone near you. It may be time for you to embark on a period of solitude. That may mean a breakup or divorce or just a refocusing of thought and effort. If your relationships are not contributing to your happiness and progress, take a step back. When combined with one of the big romance cards such as the Two of Cups or the Lovers, you and a loved one may be entering a phase of shared solitude. Sometimes we have the energy to engage with the world more broadly, and at other times we just need to make our lives very small and focused. If you are finding yourself exhausted by social interactions or excessively taxed by the demands of others, take a time-out; the world will still be here when you get back.

The reversed Hermit can indicate a negative kind of isolation. It may mean that you have withdrawn from the world because of depression, defeatism, or resentment. When you see this card in the future position, especially with a strong card like the Chariot ruling your reading, the indication is that your current actions or ambitions are alienating you from others and that you are damaging relationships. On the other hand, this card can urge you to focus on yourself and your own development rather than on the other people in your life. Are you taking enough time for personal reflection, healing, or study?

———————◆———————

THE WHEEL OF FORTUNE

Keywords: cycles, acceptance, success, failure, change,
new beginnings, perseverance, chance

The Wheel of Fortune can be a cryptic and complex card. It reminds us of the cycles of life, of success and failure, love and loss. This card urges us to practice acceptance when we are faced with things that we do not have power over. However, it also tells us to seize opportunities and make the best use of our resources. This card, unlike most, does not feature a central character; it's not about an archetype. Instead, the wheel is about the journey, about time itself and the nature of change.

In a reading the Wheel of Fortune speaks of the cyclical nature of things and this can be applied in business, work, and financial readings. Maybe you have suffered a recent loss, demotion, or failure. Or perhaps you are feeling on top of the world and things couldn't be better. Either way, the Wheel of Fortune keeps spinning, and we too must continue to move forward and challenge ourselves. Like everything else in life, relationships go through cycles. We are sometimes very close to others and find it easy to give and receive love, and other times it can feel like drawing water from a dry well. This card reminds us that these fluctuations are entirely normal.

The Wheel of Fortune reversed is always hard to see. It indicates setbacks, difficulty, or what we often think of as bad luck. You may be entering a time where things feel stacked against you, and you will have to accept a certain amount of failure, loss, or pain. At times, the Wheel of Fortune reversed warns us that there are external negative forces or people influencing our journey. Pay close attention to conflict cards in your reading as they may indicate trouble being deliberately caused. You can always regain control of your life, whether you are dealing with the failure of a marriage or bankruptcy or a loss that feels like the end of the world. As long as you are still breathing, you can reassert your will. Welcome change; try to find ways to accept the things that are happening and find the new opportunities in them.

———◆———

JUSTICE

Keywords: law, karma, fairness, justice,
honesty, balance, reason, consequences

Justice is the card that represents our desire for order, balance, and truth. For any society to run smoothly, we must have rule of law—consequences to our actions, social contracts. In a reading, the Justice card often indicates a time when the accounts—physical or karmic—must be balanced. You may be on the verge of a major decision or at a crossroad in life, a point when you need to weigh the various things that are influencing your journey forward. Sometimes this card is a warning that your actions will have consequences. This can be a positive message for a querent who feels they have worked hard for little reward. Take heart; the seeds you have planted will bear fruit eventually.

In work, business, or financial readings, Justice reminds us of the checks and balances we need for a business or creative venture to run smoothly. We often see this card when decision-making is required or when something in our lives needs attention, mediation, or a solution. Justice is an important and influential card in love, relationship, and friendship readings. It often appears when we are making important decisions or when our actions will have major impact on our future. For example, you may see this card when you are about to propose marriage or file for divorce; either way, Justice asks us to carefully weigh each influencing factor and make the decision judiciously. Justice represents the ability to see the true nature of people and their intentions. Highly intuitive people will especially understand this aspect of the card.

Reversed, Justice indicates actions that will have negative consequences. There is a warning being offered, especially when you see this card in the future position. Your current actions are going to result in a negative outcome. This may indicate that you are behaving with dishonesty or unfairness, but it may also warn you against naivety or alert you to an unsound investment. Especially when combined with conflict cards, Justice in reverse may indicate that someone is actively working against you or is being unfair to you in some way. You may see this card if you have been unwilling to examine the truth of a situation or accept responsibility for your actions.

———————◆———————

THE HANGED MAN

Keywords: crossroads, decisions, potential growth, discernment, change, letting go

The Hanged Man is the card of decisions, crossroads, and being at a standstill. The upside-down wolf-man in the Otherkin deck is suspended from a tree, his arms are crossed in a position that can be seen as either passive or defensive. This Hanged Man is a powerful character that is neither man nor wolf but something in between, which represents the middle state that this card embodies. Despite his somewhat extreme pose, his expression is relaxed. His right foot is bound to the tree, but his left foot remains free, bent at the knee. The bent leg indicates his potential for action. He can wait … or he can act. In a reading, we tend to favor movement when this card appears, especially when there are action cards such as wands present. Other times—for example, when paired with a High Priestess or Hermit— we are urged to spend time in introspection.

In a work or financial reading, the Hanged Man often reflects important decisions and approaching changes. This card pops up at times when a radical crossroad is approaching and you need to pick a road or suspend action and carefully plan your next step. Whether you are moving forward or standing still, this card encourages you to seriously consider and carefully plan your next move as it will have major impact on your life. In personal relationships, this card can indicate an end to a period of indecision or an approaching crossroad. Many relationships reach a Hanged Man phase when they are stable and healthy. That stability can be a platform for progress in other areas of the querent's life. There are times when the Hanged Man counsels acceptance. There are things in life we can control and others that will happen whether we want them to or not.

In reverse the Hanged Man may indicate that you are putting off an important decision because of fear, cowardice, or sloth. It can also mean that you are at a standstill because of something outside your control. For example, if you are caring for a young child or a sick parent, you may have to put your plans aside for a period of time. And in reverse, the indication may be that the standstill has begun to breed resentment or discontent. You may need to find small ways to work on your personal goals even if you are currently unable to extricate yourself from a frustrating situation. If you believe your own goals and dreams are on hold because of external realities or internal issues, figure out how you can make progress within your current constraints.

———◆———

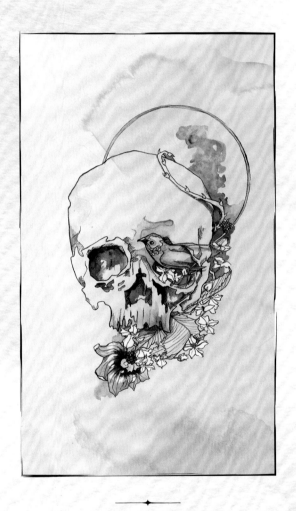

DEATH

Keywords: change, transformation, renewal,
endings, loss, liberation, growth

When the Death card shows up in a reading, it is often met with fear or shock. And though sometimes the transitions this card foretells involve pain or loss, the spirit of this card is about growth and opportunity rather than pain. This card urges you to let go of the things in your life that are holding you back. The illustration is simple: a skull from which flowers grow. In the hollow of the skull a little bird has made her home. Like the Wheel of Fortune, this card reminds us of the cycles of life and teaches us to accept things we cannot change. However, acceptance is just part of what Death teaches us. It also offers opportunity for growth.

In a work, business, or financial reading, this card urges you to welcome change and see it as a positive and transformative force. You may see this card following a loss or failure, and it should be received as a positive affirmation, a consoling omen that speaks of letting change happen, letting go of unhealthy attachments, and welcoming a fuller, more fulfilled life. In the past position the Death card indicates a loss or failure that was a fundamental moment in your life. The effects of that moment may still be unfolding. In readings about relationships, friendships, or love, the Death card unfortunately does often predict the end of something: breakups, the dissolution of a partnership, the death of a loved one, divorce. However, even the most difficult transition is an opportunity for growth. When this card is in the future position, it cautions us about the course we are on. Sometimes it advises us of an inevitable transition, but it can also serve as a warning—your actions in the present will result in the death of a relationship or loss of an important friendship.

Death reversed reflects a person who refuses to accept an inevitable change. Your resistance to transition may actually be keeping you from growing into a happier, healthier, more successful person. At times we cling to relationships, ideas, or jobs that are not helping us be our best selves. If you are carrying grudges, old wounds, or painful experiences, you may need to acknowledge the ways in which this is holding you back. Change can be difficult, but stagnation is a living death. The Death card indicates an opportunity for a new beginning if you choose to accept it.

———◆———

TEMPERANCE

Keywords: balance, moderation, communication,
management of resources, art, healing.

The Temperance card speaks of physical health, relationships, and our way of moving through the world. Strongly associated with water, this card is fluid and is concerned with both the spiritual, subconscious realm and the material world. Temperance is illustrated here as a mermaid with wings, a creature of both water and air. This card reminds us of the movement of water and the way in which nature is always seeking balance. Temperance may indicate that the querent needs to pay attention to something in their body that is out of balance—excessive drinking, an eating disorder, training that is leading to injury. Temperance celebrates balance in all things.

In work or financial readings, Temperance often guides us to middle ground, balance, and flexibility. If there are conflict cards in the reading, you may need to mediate between competing factions and encourage compromise. In relationship, friendship, or love readings, Temperance urges us toward cooperation, harmony, and health. This is not a card of big passions and life-changing decisions; rather, it asks you to slow down and think about balance. In new love readings, this card can indicate that you have met or will meet a potential spouse who understands the value of balance. This may be someone health conscious in a positive way, a spiritual practitioner of some sort, or someone who represents both genders.

Temperance reversed is a warning: something in your life is out of balance, and it will have consequences on your happiness, health, or long-term success. There may be a specific conflict or excess that is creating stress and tension in your life; for example, fighting with your spouse about money or dealing with an addiction or a difficult child. There is an indication that elements outside your control are affecting your ability to maintain balance and stability.

———◆———

THE DEVIL

Keywords: bondage, obsession, temptation, materialism,
addiction, lust, depression, attachment, independence

A card we never relish seeing, the Devil speaks of bondage, addiction, denial, and darkness. Traditionally this card features a goat or satyr and people below him in chains. Those traditional images indicate that your bondage is external—the powerful satyr looming above you is depicted as a captor and is responsible for your plight. However, this card has a message that is less about the influence of others and more about your own desires, habits, and addictions. You are your own captor, and ultimately you are also the only one that can choose freedom. In this illustration we see a female faun closely, even intimately entangled with a demon. Her head lolls compliantly to the side and her bared breast and coltish posture indicate sensuality; she shows no resistance. She is embraced by this demon; there is no struggle evident. One tendril of the demon's form covers the faun's eyes—this detail of the illustration brings attention to the fact that often we are blind to our own actions and patterns of behavior that keep us from moving forward and being our best selves. We often surrender to addictions and negative behaviors because they are familiar and can be pleasurable.

In work, professional, or financial readings, the Devil can indicate that we are committed to an old way of doing things that is no longer serving our purpose. We may feel tied to an organization, partnership, or business that is not benefiting us but that we cannot seem to break free from. Whether it is habit, fear, or dependency, something is holding you back. This card most often speaks of bondage and carries a negative connotation, but it may instead be telling you to strike out on your own, seek independence, or break with an organization. In relationship, friendship, and love readings, we see this card when there is a co-dependent relationship or one in which the partnership is not equal. Addictions such as alcoholism, sex, or gambling may be taking a toll on a friendship or relationship. In love readings, especially when there is someone new in the picture, this card can represent someone other than the querent; a rogue soul, an entrepreneur, or independent operator. This should not necessarily be seen as negative. While adherence to the rules and respect for authority can be good, the daring iconoclasts of the world are often the pioneers and groundbreakers. If that describes you, dear querent, take pride in your independent spirit and seek relationships with people who will value you rather than try to change you.

In reverse this card speaks strongly of things that are holding you back, bonds that must be broken, or addictions that are out of control. If you are overwhelmed by something, you may see the reversed Devil card appear; for example, when debt or a bad relationship have become a force that is drowning out the more positive aspects of your life. Be aware that this card may show up as a representation of someone else's struggle. The Devil reversed may indicate that they are in the grip of a strong demon such as a gambling problem, opiate addiction, or out-of-control sexual behavior. In a reading the Devil, upright or reversed, can indicate that the time has come to break negative bonds.

———————◆———————

THE TOWER

Keywords: upheaval, change, disruption, liberation,
catastrophe, divine intervention, drama, life changes

Of the seventy-eight cards in a tarot deck, the Tower is commonly thought of as the most powerful. It can be the harbinger of great change, transition, loss, and upheaval. It is important to remember that even if this card foretells difficulties ahead, you can prepare yourself to meet changes with grace and an open mind. The Otherkin version of this card depicts a lighthouse tower above a turbulent sea. The Tower itself represents the structures in your life that you have come to think of as stable, steadfast, and certain. While the foundations of this tower are holding firm against the encroaching waves the structure of the lighthouse itself is in flames. In the background a human figure is either falling from the tower or jumping into the waves to avoid the fire. This image is grim; the things you have built are on fire and you may feel like you are going to drown. The sea, while turbulent and possibly overwhelming, is also a symbol of adventure and new horizons. If you find yourself in new waters after a major upheaval or revelation, remember that struggling is what will pull you down. Relax, tread water, take slow breaths, and let yourself be carried by the waves. When you have gathered your strength and reoriented yourself, take stock of where you are. Maybe you will swim for shore and abandon your past or maybe you will see what can be salvaged and rebuild your tower. Either way, see these events as an opportunity for growth, change, and progress.

When the Tower is in a professional, work, or financial reading, it indicates a major shake-up or restructuring. Try to see even the most challenging transitions as opportunities. In relationship readings, the Tower card can foretell big changes such as marriage, childbirth, or a new person moving into your home. These changes may be very positive, but they can still be difficult to adjust to. As the Death card teaches, change brings new opportunities and room for growth; keep that in mind when the Tower is active in your life. Aside from physical changes such as the loss of a job or the death of a loved one, the Tower may represent information such as a shocking or unpleasant revelation that will change the way you see things.

Reversed, the Tower card holds a strong message for those who may be resisting a needed upheaval or putting off pain, discomfort, or humiliation necessary for the querent to pass through before they can move on to the next phase of their journey. In short, a Tower card can be a difficult thing to see in a reading, but it is also the card that holds the most potential. While you may not be able to prevent upheaval, you can prepare: try to approach things with an open mind, an open heart, and a willingness to move forward.

───────◆───────

THE STAR

Keywords: hope, blessings, good fortune, renewal,
abundance, recovery, generosity, humility, intuition, faith

The Star is a lovely, gentle card that can predict a time of positive transformation, forgiveness, and healing. In this deck she is depicted as half woman, half bird, a creature between states and in touch with the elements of air, earth, and water. This is not a card that holds fire. Although fire is a transformative element, this card speaks of gentler things. The Star often indicates that the time has come to let go of old grievances, heal old wounds, and care for yourself. More than any of the other elements, water is the key to this card. The astrological sign of the Star is Aquarius and is very connected to water, the subconscious, and emotional depth.

In a business or financial reading, this is a wonderful omen for success and personal empowerment. The Star indicates an inward focus and that can carry over to your professional and creative life. In a relationship or friendship reading, this card urges us to let go of grievances, grudges, and past offenses and to remember that we all make mistakes. Forgiving yourself and letting go of past mistakes or losses may be the first step to needed growth and the development of stronger relationships. This card often appears after conflict or following a time of intensity and reminds us that self-care and rest are important aspects of progress.

When this card appears in reverse, it serves as a gentle reminder that holding on to grudges, negativity, or even grief can hold us back. Sometimes we just have to let go of things that are not helping us be our best selves. Reflect on what internal processes are not aiding you—maybe that is negative self-talk or a lack of gratefulness. Maybe you are clinging to a past offense or keeping a grievance alive in a way that is only wounding you. Let yourself heal, be kind to yourself and others, accept change, and know that mistakes and failures are part of the journey.

THE MOON

Keywords: intuition, dreams, imagination,
deception, fear, illusion, inspiration, confusion

The Moon represents illusion, intuition, and the unconscious realm. This card most often appears in a reading when you feel uncertain, at an artistic standstill, or have lost your way. This card represents those dark moments when fears and insecurities are the loudest in your head. Take heart, though—you can emerge from this valley of shadows, and often it is these exact moments that lead to the greatest breakthroughs.

The Moon in a work or financial reading speaks of confusion, a lack of clarity, or a period of time when you are having trouble seeing your way forward. You may have reached a point where you need to question the very foundations of your life. What do you believe in? What do you truly care about? Are you on the right path or do you need to radically change direction? In friendship, relationship, or love readings, the Moon is a harbinger of confusion, bewilderment, and anxiety. You may have recently met someone promising but can't get an accurate read on their interest or investment in you. In established partnerships or friendships, you may feel disconnected from the other person and unable to communicate with them. The Moon can appear when you have everything you thought you wanted but feel unfulfilled or unable to commit. When you enter the valley of the Moon, often it is because something in your life is out of alignment with your heart's true desires. The only way out of this valley is through it. This means engaging deeply with your inner self, confronting illusions and desires, and making hard choices. This state, though difficult, can lead to enormous emotional breakthroughs. If the darkness gets the best of you, this card warns of trouble—fear, addiction, and even madness.

The Moon in reverse can indicate that you have been unwilling to confront yourself or be honest about your needs. You are stuck in confusion, turmoil, and deception because the other option—radical honesty and change—seems too painful and difficult. This card can indicate periods of hopelessness, depression, and mental illness. There may be deep emotional or psychological issues that need to be dealt with. As with the upright meaning, the reversed Moon can indicate difficulty in love relationships. If you feel your confusion is the direct result of someone else's actions, listen to your intuition. Upright or reversed, this card often advises taking a break from work or relationships in order to reconnect with your inner wisdom. There are times when you need to seek help. Please reach out to a professional or trusted ally if you feel like you are drowning in the dark.

———————◆———————

THE SUN

Keywords: joy, prosperity, acceptance, ease,
materialism, optimism, achievement, friendship

The Sun is a joyful card and is always an omen of positivity, success, abundance, and fun. Like the summer arriving after a dark and rainy spring, this card reminds you of life's simple blessings and joys. This is an overwhelmingly positive though sometimes superficial energy. It is not a complex card that speaks of deep states, long-term plans, or motivations; rather, it indicates that people will be drawn to you and that friendship, ease, and success are yours to enjoy. This card's traditional symbol, the sunflower, is a cheerful, fun flower that feeds birds and bees and brightens kitchen tables. The Sun card should be accepted for what it is: simple, uncomplicated, positive.

In work, financial, or business situations, this card urges you to say yes—yes to opportunity, yes to collaboration, yes to setting and smashing new goals. Channel this positive energy and take full advantage of the opportunities presented to you. You are asked to believe in yourself and have confidence because now is your time to shine! At the same time, while positive and energetic, the Sun is not a card that represents deep or long-lasting elements. It should be appreciated for what it is: a bright sunny day where things will go your way. Be aware that sunshine promotes growth but can also kill without the depth of water and the nurture of soil. As with everything, greet this card gratefully but with prudence. In love, relationship, or friendship readings, the Sun is a wonderful gift of fun, friendship, and joy. It is not a card with deep roots or profound effects; however, it is a blessing that may indicate a fling, a one-night stand, or simply a fun flirtation or exchange. It's okay to enjoy these moments without having to make them part of a future plan. In established partnerships, the Sun can indicate an opportunity for bonding or a period of renewed sexual energy. This invigorating card also nurtures friendships and community relationships.

In reverse the Sun warns against hyperactivity, illusions, and the superficial. While it is fine to party and enjoy material things, your journey will suffer if you make fun the sole focus of your life. This card cautions us against spreading ourselves too thin, overcommitting, or trying to be everywhere at once. Without focus, you will not accomplish lasting security or success. If your endeavors and relationships are based on superficiality, they will wither away when adversity arrives.

◆

JUDGMENT

Keywords: awakening, vocation, enlightenment,
progression, absolution, rebirth

The Judgment card is the clear note of a horn that shatters the quiet and rouses you from sleep. It announces an epiphany or awakening and urges you toward a period of self-evaluation and change. Often this card appears for people who have a calling, a strong inclination to be of service to others, or who are in pursuit of a difficult goal. These urges often get pushed down and ignored as you struggle to find stability, financial success, or fulfill obligations to others. You may see this card because your journey has come to a point of maturity and understanding, Judgment indicates that you may finally be ready to follow your dreams.

The Judgment card in work readings often speaks of a coming transition or opportunity for transformation. The Judgment card heralds service to others, deep passions, and the actualization of our inner selves. This card tells you that it is possible to lead a life that fulfills your dreams and offers inspiration and hope to others. In the illustration for this card, a bear holds a horn that sounds the battle cry; below is a single egg just beginning to crack, a symbol of awakening. The Judgment card in relationship readings indicates the potential for new possibilities and transformative energy. Unburden yourself of old baggage; let go of negativity, resentment, and old relationships—this is a new day and a new opportunity to rise to greatness. If you are at the beginning of a new relationship, don't be afraid to forge forward with an open heart. In established relationships, a common goal or calling may reinvigorate and deepen an existing bond. Listen to your heart. Choose friendships, partnerships, and lovers that align with your deep beliefs and passions. The Judgment card often arrives when you realize that you have not been living up to your potential.

Judgment in reverse indicates self-doubt, reticence, or cowardice. Your fear of failure may be preventing you from following your dreams. You may long to be of service to others but feel unable to take the necessary steps to move forward toward a new life. Indecision or codependency may be holding you back; this card warns that the time has come to move forward as your opportunities may not be available much longer. Channel the energy of the Fool in your life, take a new journey, be daring, and follow the call of Judgment's trumpet—it is time for you to rise.

———————◆———————

THE WORLD

Keywords: end of a cycle, victory, achievement, goals,
travel, success, completion, fulfillment

The last card in the major arcana, the World symbolizes completion, achievement, and fulfillment. A cycle is ending, and it is time to welcome a new phase of life. The symbols for Leo, Taurus, Aquarius, and Scorpio are represented in the four corners of this card as they symbolize the four elements and the four seasons. In the present position, this card is an affirmation of the hard work and effort you have invested in something. Even if you are still in the thick of a battle, know that your reward will soon manifest. The World urges us to embrace the new opportunities and responsibilities that come with each new cycle.

In work, financial, or professional readings, this card indicates changes, transitions, and things coming to an end. This may mean the end of your current job or position or a much-deserved promotion that will offer opportunities for growth. Remember that every ending is also a beginning, so ask yourself: What new horizon is calling you? In relationship or friendship readings, this card represents endings, closure, and life transitions. It could signify a divorce, a marriage, the birth of a child, or a major milestone that you or a loved one has accomplished. You may be thrust into a time of transition upon having finally accomplished a goal or completed a large endeavor. The World speaks about those moments and about what comes next for you and how these cycles affect your relationships. Take time to celebrate and acknowledge how far you have come! Embrace change and allow yourself to see all the opportunity this next phase of life has made available to you.

In reverse this card speaks of a cycle not completed. It may indicate unfinished projects or unresolved issues, It may suggest that you are resisting change or refusing to let something go even though you know it is over. At times this card will alert you to the actions of others. Whether you are holding yourself back or something external is preventing you from moving forward, you must work toward a resolution if you wish to continue to grow and prosper.

———————◆———————

CHAPTER 3

MINOR ARCANA

The Journey Continues

THE SUIT OF CUPS
We move upon the waters

———◆———

The suit of cups speaks to us of the flow of creativity, intuition, and emotion. Here are the cards that instruct us in the realm of emotional relationships and help us maximize our artistic powers. When your query is about love, friendship, and intuition, these are the cards you will most often see. The element embodied in this suit is that of water. Partnerships and marriages are represented by the Two of Cups while the Three of Cups address group dynamics and friendships. The Seven of Cups speaks of wishful thinking and illusions, and the Five of Cups of disappointment and negativity. In general, all of these cards speak of internal states, emotions, our bonds with other people, and the ways in which our life choices are affecting our creativity. Where swords represent the intellect or wands call for action, the c,ups often urge us toward stillness, contemplation, and a focus on our feelings. There is a self-care aspect to this suit and a profound emphasis on the emotional and creative.

ACE OF CUPS

*Keywords: awakening, love, new opportunities,
learning, new potential, new beginnings*

The Ace of Cups is the feminine counterpoint to the masculine Ace of Wands. This card is the gentle offering of new beginnings, self-development, and relationships. Drawing on the subconscious realm and the world of feeling and intuition, the Ace of Cups often speaks of spiritual, emotional, or creative growth and opportunity. Almost all depictions of this card involve a cup, chalice, or other vessel that is overflowing with water. This imagery is a reminder of the ways in which we hold creativity and intuition and that to take full advantage of these powers in the universe, we have to let them flow freely. The fish represents the forces of creativity and intuition and ties this card to others that channel artistic energy, such as the Queen of Cups.

In a professional or financial reading, this card often speaks of new opportunities in the creative realm that will push you to grow in new ways. This card is not about the analytical or technical, but rather it places emphasis on your intuition and creativity when faced with problems or challenges. In a love or relationship reading, it often indicates a new romance or a new phase in an existing relationship. You may be presented with an opportunity to connect in a meaningful way that will feed your creativity and promote spiritual or emotional growth. It often indicates new life, a child, pregnancy, or even a new pet.

In reverse the Ace of Cups often cautions the querent about letting their emotions get the best of them. Jealousy, resentment, or hurt feelings may be preventing you from reaching your full potential. Allowing other people's drama to affect your life is also a concern. Creativity and intuition can be adversely affected by others, especially when they bring chaos or negative energy to your life.

———————◆———————

TWO OF CUPS

Keywords: marriage, relationships, partnership,
common goals, friendship, contracts

This card speaks of the wonderful potential held in the bonds between people. Sometimes that bond is romance, marriage, and physical relationships but just as often it speaks of friendship, partnership, and situations in which you share goals, projects, or ideas with another person. Even a significant friendship with an animal can be addressed by the Two of Cups.

In a professional or financial reading, the Two of Cups speaks most clearly of partnerships. This may mean starting a business with a significant other or forming a strong working relationship with a colleague. Is there a page or ace in your reading? Those cards often speak of something new: an opportunity, a new partner, or a new relationship that has potential to blossom into something significant.

In a romance or friendship reading, the Two of Cups often shows up when there is a deep bond between two people that love and respect each other. An important aspect to consider when you see this card in a reading is that of self-development and enlightenment. Do you crave a deep relationship or want to find the perfect business partner but notice that kind of friendship has eluded you? The Two of Cups may be indicating that you have personal, internal work to do before you will be ready to be a great partner.

The Two of Cups reversed often speaks of a bond that has been broken. Has there been a betrayal, dishonesty, or other action that has undermined an important relationship? What action can you take to begin the work of repair? If you or your partner have broken the bond, take sometime to think deeply not just about how to fix things but to what the underlying causes of the rupture are.

———◆———

THREE OF CUPS

*Keywords: friendship, community, social events,
celebration, fun, group dynamics*

The Three of Cups is a fun card that addresses friendship, interpersonal dynamics, and celebration. It can urge you to participate more in your community or it can simply remind you how valuable friendships are and how much they bring to your life.

In a business, financial, or professional type reading, this card reminds us of the value of camaraderie. If you are considering or querying about a new situation, this card may indicate something in the social sphere—event planning, for example, or another job that involves working with people. The Three of Cups can indicate that you will soon join a new team. This is an interesting card to see in a romance reading as it can mean that your love is already among your close group of friends or that friendship is a significant influencer in your current relationship dynamics. If you are seeking a mate, look more closely at those in your community. This card can pop up when folks are seeking romance but the deck wants to remind you to tend to your friendships rather than focus on romance at this time. The Three of Cups can sometimes apply to open or polyamorous relationships.

In reverse the Three of Cups most notoriously speaks of the classic love triangle. Is it possible that your love interest seems distracted because they are emotionally or physically engaged with someone else? Like most things in tarot, introspection and balance are indicated. Is there a Hermit in your reading? You may need some time alone to figure out your priorities and how to best use your social energy.

FOUR OF CUPS

Keywords: isolation, negativity, denial, self-indulgence,
moodiness, lack of vision, turning inward, depression

In the Otherkin deck, the Four of Cups is pictured as an octopus. The octopus has eight arms, a symbol of all the industry this creature is capable of, but each of these arms is curled up on itself, an indication that the octopus is not participating in the world. The human equivalent would be sitting on your hands or standing with your arms crossed. The octopus in this drawing is also hiding under a lily pad and has its eyes tightly shut. It is hiding away, not engaging with the world and not seeing what is going on. This card may indicate that you or someone close to you has sunk into a place of despair, denial, or even full-on depression.

In a professional, financial, or work reading, this card can appear when the querent is discouraged, bored, or feels unseen in their current situation. You may need to find a new job, position, or team where you are appreciated. It's very difficult to initiate change when you are in this state, but if you remain here, things will only grow worse. The Four of Cups can suggest a time of deep introspection or self-involvement—this can be especially true for creative folks. When it appears in a love, friendship, or relationship context, the Four of Cups may indicate that you are feeling disengaged, apathetic, or bored. Sometimes we see the Four of Cups when a querent is seeking love but is more focused on their needs and past wounds and has not done necessary internal work that would open them up to the possibility of a significant friendship or romantic bond. At other times this card offers a suggestion: look inward, find affirmation and value in yourself rather than in others.

This card in reverse presents a strong message. The negative aspect of the card generally speaks of someone, either the querent or someone significant in their lives, who has embraced negativity, depression, illness, or boredom, and is allowing it to control their lives or define their identity. We all have times of difficulty, depression, anxiety, pain—grace is moving through it and accepting it as part of life while not letting it become who we are.

———————◆———————

FIVE OF CUPS

*Keywords: grief, despair, negative thinking,
loss, pessimism vs optimism*

The Five of Cups indicates a need to shift our focus toward the positive and put our efforts into changing those things we have power over instead of obsessing about loss, difficulty, or pain. The image on this card is of a mer-woman crying over broken eggs. Two of the eggs are broken while three are still standing. Her focus is on grief and loss instead of remembering that there are still things in life to celebrate and indeed places where her energy is desperately needed. While loss and grief are part of life, this card is a reminder of how vital our outlook is and how much it shapes our world. In the Thoth Tarot this card is called Lord of Disappointment, and if it is in the future position in a reading it can indicate that you should prepare for some degree of disappointment or disillusionment.

This card tends to appear more frequently in love or relationship readings but can be very relevant to professional and financial matters as well. Have you experienced a financial setback or professional failure or difficulty? Are you struggling within your work life to find a sense of purpose and have become focused on the things that are missing instead of those that are present? If you are seeing this card in a past position, it can indicate that past failures or losses are preventing you from taking a chance on something that could really help you blossom and move forward. Sometimes this card just speaks to you about perspective and a change in the way you see the world. Try to focus on the positive, on the things that can be helped rather than the overwhelming number of things that can't be changed.

In reverse the Five of Cups can indicate a profound or long-lasting sense of loss or general disappoint in life. It can also mean that the querent is struggling to accept something difficult that is beyond their control. Another aspect of this card, especially in the past position, is that the disappointment is behind you or that you have understood that loss, grief, or failure are part of the journey and have made your peace with that.

SIX OF CUPS

Keywords: childhood, nostalgia, reunion,
happiness, memories, teaching, generosity

The Six of Cups is a sweet card that speaks of nostalgia, childhood, and good memories. For the Otherkin deck, I chose to draw a loving mermaid and child. Their calm expressions and relaxed, protective posture indicate all the feelings one has (or wishes they had) regarding parent-child relationships and the good energy of a loving home. There can be a degree of immaturity indicated with this card or a stubborn reluctance to grow up and take responsibility. This card can also indicate an event, a reunion with childhood friends, or a weekend with your parents, for example.

In a work, professional, or financial reading, this card can indicate unwise spending that may be negatively impacting your current financial situation. Often it implies that the querent (or someone close to them) is operating with a degree of irresponsibility, childishness, or the expectation that things will just work out. Nostalgia is an important word that comes up with this card. Sometimes it means you are attempting to recreate a feeling or environment that no longer serves you, but often it can indicate that your strength comes from your past and is grounded in specific people or feelings from childhood, especially when the card is in the past position. In a love or relationship/friendship reading, the Six of Cups can represent a return to a familiar environment or feeling. It can be a situation where you end up dating someone quite similar to a parental figure, or it can indicate a certain childishness and lack of depth. It can also be positive and can mean that you are with someone or will be with someone who makes you feel safe and protected.

The Six of Cups reversed may indicate a reluctance to let go of certain ideas about the world that are rooted in childish expectation, especially in the past position. It often shows up when folks are pining for children and are having difficulty conceiving. Codependency can also be indicated. If you are in a relationship or even a work situation where you are playing the child, it may be time for you to step up and take on leadership roles.

————————◆————————

SEVEN OF CUPS

*Keywords: ideas, mystery, thoughts,
illusions, dreams, distractions, mystery*

The Seven of Cups speaks of illusions, dreams, mystery, and expectations. The image on this card is usually that of a figure contemplating a variety of cups that hold objects—a snake, a ring, jewels, a mountain, and so on. These objects symbolize the various things that distract us or that we desire, but they can also represent our fears or anxieties. The message of this card is twofold: on the one hand it cautions against letting imagination dominate our reality, yet it also speaks of the value of dreams, aspiration, and vision.

In a financial or professional reading, the message this card holds can be very practical. Say you long for financial security or freedom: the advice would be to save, invest, pay down debt, stick to a budget, and so on. This card urges us toward these kinds of practical measures and away from the realm of the imaginary—for example, saving and investing rather than pinning your hopes on a lottery ticket. Our daydreams can be very informative—perhaps you find yourself fantasizing about owning your own yoga studio, for example. Rather than dismissing that thought, give it some real consideration. Write a business plan, and figure out what you need to do to make it an actual possibility. *Focus* is another message this card holds. If we are constantly distracted by new projects, it can be very difficult to get substantial, significant work done. In relationship readings the Seven of Cups often cautions against unrealistic expectations and letting our fantasies hinder our relationships with others.

Pay careful attention to this card in reverse; it can indicate that all is not as it seems. Do you have doubts about a situation or person? Do you feel like they might be hiding something behind a glamorous or calm veneer? Look to other cards in the reading for clues about why you might be feeling this way. At times when the Seven of Cups card is reversed, it can indicate a disconnection with your dreams or imagination. This card often manifests for creative people when they are feeling blocked or unable to work freely.

———◆———

EIGHT OF CUPS

Keywords: moving on, travel, new ideas,
severing ties, change, leaving, adventure

The Eight of Cups speaks to us of transitions and moving on. Sometimes this may mean leaving a situation and sometimes it indicates a more interior change, like a shift in perspective or goals. Often when this card appears in a reading the querent is at a cross-roads. The Eight of Cups generally features a solitary figure with their back turned to the viewer. The figure on the card embodies a feeling of departure; they are walking away from something. In the Otherkin Tarot, a selkie stands in the water with her back turned to us. On a rock behind her is an overturned cup that symbolizes the things the querent is considering leaving behind. I chose a selkie for this card because they represent a liminal state, the sense of being between things—water and land, staying and leaving. In this version the querent is not completely alone; in the water around her are the bobbing heads of a few water friends, a reminder that though you may feel alone and afraid, you are not.

Here is a card that heralds change, transition, and leaving, so it's no surprise that we often see it when the querent is wondering about professional or job-related questions, especially if they are pondering leaving a job or situation. The quandary with the Eight of Cups is that it often appears when the querent is dissatisfied and contemplating change; it can be difficult to know when to quit and when to persevere. In a relationship, romance, or friendship reading, the Eight of Cups generally addresses breakups, divorce, or exiting a friendship. We must sometimes persist and be patient because all good relationships require work and compromise, but it is also important to recognize when a relationship is no longer serving us or the other party.

The Eight of Cups reversed often speaks to a querent who has been stuck in a state of vagueness, dissatisfaction, or disillusionment and has been unwilling to move forward. It can also indicate someone who moves on too quickly and can't focus or commit. To get anything done, a certain amount of tenacity and focus is required. If you quit every time you feel bored or dissatisfied, you won't accomplish anything. These are the two extremes this card represents, the quitter/flake who won't put in the work and the querent who is too afraid of the unknown to make necessary changes. Dare yourself to move toward a better life, whether that means committing to a course of action or walking away to new horizons.

NINE OF CUPS

Keywords: wish fulfillment, good luck,
promotion, rewards, happiness

The Nine of Cups is a happy, positive card that speaks of wish fulfillment, good luck, and things going our way. Even when paired with less positive cards, this message is still quite clear: the thing you are hoping for is within your grasp. However, granted wishes have a flip side. Perhaps you get what you wanted but discover afterward that it brings undesirable elements to your life.

In a work, professional, or financial situation, the Nine of Cups heralds promotions, advancement, or monetary windfalls. In a relationship, friendship, or love reading, the Nine of Cups says that you can achieve your heart's desire. The smugness of this card makes it likely that you see news that makes you happy in a not entirely positive way; for example, you find out that your ex is getting a divorce or that a former rival has become obese. Everything associated with the Nine of Cups has two aspects; you get what you want but there is some price to pay. It may be as simple as the bellyache that comes from eating all your Halloween candy at once, but it can also speak of extramarital affairs, reconnecting with unhealthy relationships, or general overindulgence. Some caution is advised.

The Nine of Cups is a card we all like to see. The message it carries is "hey, you are going to get your way", and who doesn't want to hear that? However, it can also speak to the cost of wish fulfillment; the alienation of success, the burden of leadership, the pressure associated with visibility or recognition. In reverse the Nine of Cups carries an even stronger caution: the price of your desire may outweigh the benefit. Remember that if something seems too good to be true, it probably is.

———◆———

TEN OF CUPS

Keywords: legacy, long-term happiness, strong partnerships,
marriage, family, prosperity, positivity, joy

The Ten of Cups is sometimes called the legacy card. It is indicative of the kind of long-term success that is more about deep happiness and wellbeing than it is about specific monetary goals or outward symbols of success. This is a card that speaks to an examined life well lived, smart investments, and long-term plans. In readings it often pops up in the future position and counsels the querent toward taking the longer view of their life instead of the fastest route. The advice usually given by this card is that you should invest in the future rather than the present, whether that means continuing your education, making relationship choices, or developing an investment strategy.

When specifically looking at work or professional development, the Ten of Cups often means pursuing advanced schooling, apprenticeship, training, or staying at a job where you will learn vital things but may not be compensated as well as you would like. The question you should be weighing now is whether the choices you are pondering make for good long-term goals. In a love or relationship reading, this is one of the best cards you can see. The Ten of Cups is about long-term relationships, the deep happiness of a strong bond, and the establishment of family. This card often shows up in the influencing position in a reading, which indicates that you have this kind of relationship already and that it is a source of strength or that your desire for this kind of relationship motivates your choices. It can also mean that a strong bond is evading you for some specific reason.

In reverse the Ten of Cups often indicates that something is working against your long-term happiness and wellbeing. Sometimes the Ten of Cups reversed plainly states that your current relationship or partnership (with a person or company) is just not working and is not a match for the long haul. There are times in life when we have to let go of things in order to make room for something better.

PAGE OF CUPS

Keywords: inspiration, creativity, the unexpected,
new projects, intuition

Have you ever had a flash of inspiration come to you out of the blue? A business idea, tune, image, or new thought that strikes like lightning while you are making breakfast or walking the dog? That is the sort of inspiration that the Page of Cups speaks to. This card is a wonderful omen for new projects and ventures and indicates a time when you should keep an open mind and pay attention to the world around you. It often indicates the arrival of a message or messenger bearing good news or an invitation.

In a work or professional reading, the Page of Cups speaks most clearly of new ideas and projects. It can signal the return of inspiration which might arrive in an unexpected way. Don't shy away from things that seem outlandish or unexpected—this card tells us to welcome the unexpected and to open our minds to new possibilities. In a relationship, friendship, or love reading, the Page of Cups can mean good news arriving. For example, a positive pregnancy test, an engagement, or a message from an old friend can be indicated. The Page of Cups often shows up when a new person is about to enter our lives, someone who has the potential to bring positive changes and inspiration.

The Page of Cups in reverse can indicate that the querent or someone else in the situation is exhibiting immaturity or irresponsible behavior. We often see this card in a reading when a youthful or creative person is being flaky, dishonest, or behaving in a way that is negatively affecting the people around them. As we noted before, this card often speaks of a message or messenger or new opportunities. If this card is in reverse, it can warn that a new venture or idea may sound like great fu, but you should engage cautiously.

———◆———

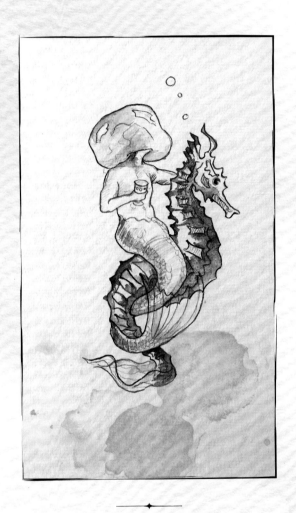

KNIGHT OF CUPS

*Keywords: romance, imagination, adventure,
creativity, emotion, enthusiasm*

The Knight of Cups is the proverbial knight in shining armor. Fun and romantic, this knight charges in full of big ideas and enthusiasm. This card can signal someone entering the querent's life who possesses these characteristics or it can represent the querent themselves. The energy of this card is creative and intuitive rather than analytical. There is an element of being out of touch with reality or having one's head in the clouds. I tried to express that idea by having this knight's head encased in a bubble. As a creative person myself, I relate very strongly to this card and to the disconnection with reality it can represent.

In a work or financial reading, the Knight of Cups can signify excessive optimism or an unrealistic view of the current situation. You may not be seeing things clearly or you might be working toward a dream or romantic ideal that is unrealistic. In a financial reading, this card can indicate that you are being overly generous with your time and resources and that it might result in feelings of disillusionment or disappointment. Do you find yourself giving too much to others and receiving little in return? Like most things in tarot, it's all about balance. We often see the knights in a love or relationship reading when new people enter our lives; a messenger, suitor, or even a new friend or co-worker. There is generally an air of romance about this card, which may signal a love connection but can also mean a friend or a possible collaborator who is artistic or emotional. When this card shows up for a querent who is in active pursuit of someone or something, the Knight of Cups counsels us toward romantic gestures, emotions, and displays of affection.

The reversed Knight of Cups can indicate that you are being overly sensitive or are allowing your feelings to drive you toward incorrect conclusions. This card may be a warning against charismatic, emotional, or artistic people who hide ill intentions behind an attractive façade. Be wary of anyone in your life who seems to be too good to be true. Read the fine print before making any new commitments—literally and metaphorically. Now is not the time for blind faith, especially if you are in a new relationship. Trust, but verify. Likewise, if you have been behaving in a not entirely upfront way, be cautious; our secrets have a way of finding their way into the light.

———————◆———————

QUEEN OF CUPS

Keywords: intuition, creativity, spirituality, fertility,
creativity, success, power, femininity

The Queen of Cups is the lovely ruler of emotion, creativity, and intuition. Many tarot readers feel a special affinity for this card because she represents that inner voice that diviners must learn (or re-learn) to hear in order to do the work. At her best this queen reminds us of the power of compassion and is a pillar of strength within her community. She inspires others to live fully and follow their own voice. Unlike the charismatic Queen of Wands, this lady does not inspire loyalty through cult of personality or fear of reprisal; instead, she shepherds people gently with love and understanding.

In a work, professional, or financial reading, the Queen of Cups reminds us of the power of creativity and the value of intuition. If you are facing challenges, take some time away from the opinions of others and find the silence you need to reconnect with your own ideas and feelings. In a love or relationship reading, the Queen of Cups represents the loving, generous energy of a mother. She is a caretaker not just of the physical plane—she also nurtures the inner strength and unique gifts of those around her. If you are having trouble in your relationship or are having difficulty connecting with others in a significant way, take some time to examine the way in which you are dealing with the world. Are you being compassionate and kind to yourself as well as to others? Are you holding space for others and helping them feel safe and valued?

The Queen of Cups reversed can be a reminder that in order for things to flow—be it love, money, or water—there must be bilateral openness. The message here is that you need to give in order to receive; you need to be open to the energy of the universe, to the love of others, to your own value. Reconnect with your intuition and inner strength. This card can sometimes indicate a serious problem within the querent (or with someone they are close to); grief, depression, or an unhealthy dependency can be stealing your power. If you need help to deal with things that are holding you back, please reach out and find your way back to the light. The world needs the love and joy you hold.

———◆———

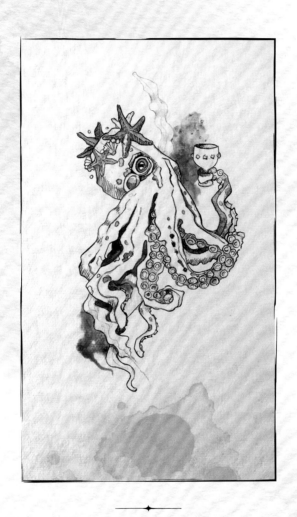

KING OF CUPS

Keywords: authority, fairness, clear vision,
maturity, intelligence, leadership

The King of Cups is the regal ruler of emotion, creativity, and the unconscious realm. He is stable and in control and represents the balance between feelings and the intellect. He is the spirit of creative mastery, the calm and kind authority that does not need to diminish others to aggrandize himself. When he appears in a reading, it is often as a representation of someone in the querent's life—a mentor, professor, or paternal figure that has the potential to bring out the best in those around him.

In a work, professional, or financial reading, we often see this card when the querent is moving into a position of leadership or authority. The King of Cups advises a leadership style that makes others feel valued and creates space for everyone's ideas and creative input. This king values kindness, compassion, and communication, but he is still a strong voice of authority. This card can indicate an ally or an older authority figure who may be able to help you with a financial or work-related situation. In a love or relationship reading, the King of Cups represents a person in their full power, connected to their feelings and artistic gifts. He is the perfect mate and a wonderful father. If you see a king and queen card in your reading, it is an omen for the kind of relationship that is possible only between highly evolved equals.

The negative aspect of the King of Cups is most often emotional or egotistical. This card represents a powerful, talented person with a high degree of emotional range. If all those gifts are not balanced by compassion, maturity, and kindness, the result can be an enormous ego and some very bad behavior. The King of Cups reversed can wield a lot of influence over others and represent the kind of leader that inspires loyalty but also has explosions of rage, anger, or childishness. If this card represents someone in your life, look to adjacent cards for counsel about how to deal with them. There is always another job, a different relationship, a new mentor. Most importantly, remember that you do not need to put up with abusive behavior from anyone, ever, full stop.

———◆———

THE SUIT OF WANDS
Of spark, flame, and ember

———◆———

Corresponding to the element of fire, the wands represent passion, charisma, and energy. These are the cards that speak about the activities you engage in daily as well as new projects, journeys, and adventures. There is an emotional and creative aspect to these cards, but unlike the cups, wands do not celebrate the quiet concept-forming phase of creativity; they embody the excitement of sharing ideas and the implementation of plans. There are cards in the suit of wands that address competition, power struggles, and interpersonal tension. For example, the Five of Wands indicates strife or disagreement, and the Seven of Wands foretells conflict and rivalry. Wands are great to see when you are ready to move into the action phase of a project or if you are contemplating a move or journey.

The wands court cards can represent the querent themselves, especially in times of action or movement, and they can also represent powerful and charismatic people in the querent's life. They are the movers and shakers, dynamic suitors, and strong personalities. At their best, these cards are full of energy and positivity. At their worst, they are volatile, hasty, and have the potential to wound. Much like fire itself, the wands can attract and warm…but they can also burn and destroy.

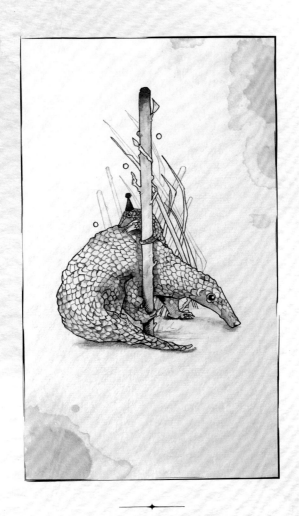

ACE OF WANDS

Keywords: new projects, ideas, enthusiasm,
cleverness, industry, luck, fertility

The Ace of Wands urges you to begin that new project, take a chance on your dreams, make a move, go on a trip. In short, this card pushes you toward action. In its upright manifestation, this ace is full of potential and growth. Like new growth bursting out of the ground in the first weeks of spring, there is both enthusiasm and an element of fragility present with this ace. A hard frost will kill new flowers, miscarriage is frequent in early pregnancy, and one person's harsh words can suck the life out of a creative venture before it even has time to develop. To use the analogy of fire, this is the spark phase of building a fire, so the new flames must be sheltered from the elements until the wood catches and the fire can burn robustly. I used a pangolin as the illustration on this card to symbolize the caution we must take when starting new things. Be bold … but wear your armor!

In a professional or financial reading, the Ace of Wands encourages you to move soon. If you have been pondering a new position, direction, or project, this is a good time to act. When there is more than one ace in a reading, the cards are giving you a big yes and maybe a little shove. The Ace of Wands shows up in love readings, especially when the relationship is new or when the querent is about to meet someone fun and dynamic. In more established relationships, this card can indicate a new phase, a journey together, a time of reinvigorated sexual interest, and pregnancy. There is a phallic procreative energy to this card, the desire to mate and reproduce.

In reverse the Ace of Wands can speak to impulsiveness, lack of planning, and things never moving past the initial phase. Miscarriage both literal and metaphorical may be foretold. This is a card we might see when enthusiasm sours. If you are on the verge of making a change or commitment, starting a new business, or making a geographical move, a reversed Ace of Wands can indicate that you need to pause and read the fine print. Take a little extra time to weigh the elements and proceed with caution.

———◆———

TWO OF WANDS

Keywords: planning, progress, travel,
new ventures, investment, foresight, enthusiasm

The visual elements most commonly associated with the Two of Wands are the globe and a character looking out at a landscape. The globe represents the world and all the possibility it holds. It signifies travel, expanded horizons, perspectives outside of our own, as well as opportunity. The character in the case of the Otherkin deck, a dapper frog, can see not just the things in front of him but the wider picture, a global view. This card reminds us to consider the vast opportunities and adventures available to us. We are also encouraged to look beyond the immediate circumstances and to plan for the future rather than the present.

In work, professional, or financial readings, the message this card holds is to expand our thinking—plan for growth and globalization. If you are seeing this card at the beginning of a new venture, you are advised to build in a scalable way. Take a global view of your endeavors, consider travel, consider what other countries, cultures, and markets have to offer. You may not be able to do everything you want immediately, but you *can* take small steps everyday toward your larger goals. Don't lose sight of the big picture! In readings that deal with love, relationships, and friendships, this card speaks of expanded horizons, travel, and long-term relationships.

Achieving your goals requires patience, saving, and putting in the hours. In reverse this card warns us about pursuing immediate gratification at the price of long-term satisfaction. We have to strike a balance between the dynamic, life-sustaining energy of a well-built fire and the impulsive, wasteful flame that only consumes and destroys. One requires planning, containment, and careful construction; the other is just the energy of potential running wild and without discipline. We often see this card in reverse when something is impeding the querent's journey. Negativity, dependency, depression, illness— these can all be elements that prevent you from acting. Look to adjacent cards for advice about the restoration of balance in your life.

———◆———

THREE OF WANDS

Keywords: partnerships, long-term plans,
organization, investment, cooperation

The Three of Wands is a great omen when you are contemplating growth and expansion. The growth indicated can be work or family related but can also signify personal development and investment in yourself. If paired with any of the aces, consider moving toward action now rather than lingering in the planning stages any longer. There is a long-term aspect to this card that admonishes us to plan for future rather than just present growth.

In work, professional, and financial readings, this card has particular relevance. The message here is long-range investment, self-development, and growth. In the Otherkin Tarot, the image on this card is of a character on a hill surveying the landscape. He has a pair of binoculars in his hand that enable him to see quite far. The visual metaphor is that we need to take the long view in our endeavors and investments. This card also encourages cooperation and partnerships. It is a good omen in a relationship reading and can indicate long-term and family-building potential or a business partnership. You may soon meet a new person or are possibly in a new relationship that has the potential to be significant. At times, this card comes up when the querent is contemplating expanding their family; it can be a good omen for pregnancy and other kinds of legacy building, such as buying a home, for example.

When you see this card in the past position, it can speak to disappointments or failures you might still be carrying. Say you were heavily invested in a relationship that you thought had future potential but ended in heartbreak. Remember that failure is part of life and that any endeavor worth pursuing comes with the risk of failure. Focus on healing and letting go of past losses so that you can move forward on your journey. At times the Three of Wands can indicate delays, obstacles, or problems that slow your progress. Be especially cautious of people who may not follow through on promises or fulfill contracts.

———◆———

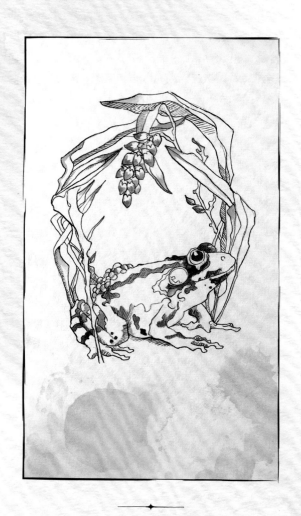

FOUR OF WANDS

Keywords: celebration, community,
happiness, family, success, prosperity

The Four of Wands is a celebratory card that speaks of community and coming together. This card often heralds marriages, graduations, and new births. Overwhelmingly positive and gentle, the message here is a reminder of your value to others and your place within a community. This card can also indicate the arrival of a positive message or windfall.

In a work or financial reading, the Four of Wands can indicate prosperity and cause for celebration. A bit of luck or generous return on investment may manifest at this time. You may see this card upon the completion of a project or even the end of your tenure at a particular job or position, such as retirement or graduation. This card reminds us to celebrate the things we have been through while still remembering that the future is full of potential. Sometimes real estate dealings can be indicated with this card as it has a heavy association with the home and homebuilding. In the Otherkin Tarot, the frog in the illustration is carrying eggs on its back and is happily nested under a canopy of leaves and flowers. This card often appears when we are in a nesting mode or when the focus needs to be on home and family. If you are looking for relationship advice, this card speaks to the sense of home that some people have for the familiar and cozy rather than the high energy or crazy unknown.

In reverse the Four of Wands can indicate that you are feeling displaced, unsettled, or out of sorts. Your sense of belonging—or indeed, your actual home—is suffering from tension or disruption. Perhaps the end of a cycle has arrived and you are struggling to accept it. If you see a reversed Death card or a Hanged Man, the cards may be encouraging you to accept a needed transition and take steps toward the future.

———◆———

FIVE OF WANDS

Keywords: rivalry, tension, bickering, competition,
challenges, standing up for yourself, chaos

The Five of Wands speaks of conflict, competition, and bickering caused by differences of opinion or lack of leadership. The antidote is clear communication and precise goal setting. If there are many voices, you might need to take a step back and consider the opinions and perspectives of others. In the past position, unresolved conflict may be driving current tensions.

We often see the Five of Wands in work readings when chaos or conflict are affecting your ability to meet goals or enjoy your work. There is an element of chaos represented, and it may be that disorganization within the querent themselves or trouble focusing is part of the problem. You may need to set aside some time to set goals and get organized. While competition in the workplace can sometimes lead to productivity, it is seldom welcome at home. In a relationship or friendship reading, the Five of Wands can indicate bickering, power struggles, and discontent. Create space for clear communication and be ready to address grievances. To be a good partner, communicate with clarity about your goals and boundaries while still being open to compromise.

The Five of Wands reversed can indicate that you or someone in your life is creating tension or chaos. It is possible that you are not handling conflict well or that you are creating issues instead of resolving them. Though this card has more of a chaotic spirit rather than a sneaky one, in reverse it can sometimes mean that someone is stirring up trouble behind your back. For example, if a person is attempting to woo someone you have expressed romantic interest in or if a work rival is spreading lies or acting in a way that would make others distrust you, the Five of Wands reversed might offer insight.

SIX OF WANDS

Keywords: recognition, awards,
accomplishment, praise, pride, fame

The Six of Wands is a happy card that almost always means the querent has cause to celebrate. The illustration for the Otherkin deck features a chameleon perched on a branch with a look of contentment on his face. He is wearing a little crown of laurel and has an air of triumph. Recognition, visibility, and appreciation are foretold by this card. The message in this reading may simply be to continue working because soon your work will be acknowledged.

In professional, work, or financial readings, this card speaks of promotions and recognition, awards and rewards. These may come as a pat on the back from a team leader, a good evaluation, or a contract or bonus. Whatever the delivery method, the message is clear: you are doing a good job and have reason to be proud of yourself. If you have been contemplating starting your own business or taking on more responsibility, consider making that transition soon. In a personal or relationship reading, this card can indicate that your visibility and accomplishments will make you attractive to others. Look for other folks that are on a similar trajectory, people focused on self-improvement and goal attainment; you will find easy friendships there. Sometimes this card can indicate that it is your role to recognize others. If your spouse or friend has accomplished something, consider ways in which you can celebrate their success and make them feel valued.

The Six of Wands reversed cautions against arrogance, self-satisfaction, and being blinded by your own light. It's healthy to be proud of our accomplishments, but we can do that *and* still keep things in perspective. No matter how awesome you are, there are other folks out there working just as hard and creating things that are just as spectacular. Nobody likes a braggart. Choose confidence and kindness over arrogance. This card also cautions against negative and self-deprecating thinking.

———◆———

SEVEN OF WANDS

Keywords: rivalry, competition, jealousy,
shadiness, backstabbers, squabbling, conflict

The Seven of Wands is also called the Lord of Valor, and it speaks to us of courage and holding our ground in the face of adversity. There is a strong element of competition associated with this card, which can mean a rival seeking to take something from you or people who are envious of your success or status.

Most often appearing in work or professional readings, this card cautions against passivity. The Six of Wands is a card about recognition and the garnering of laurels that acknowledge our hard work…and the Seven of Wands reminds us not to rest on those laurels. You may be called upon to step into roles of authority or leadership, an action that may not be met with acceptance by everyone. If you believe you are being challenged or that someone is undermining you, clear communication and the setting of boundaries is recommended. Don't let tensions and rivalries get you down. Focus on the future. Do the things that you do best and stand your ground. In a relationship reading the Seven of Wands may indicate that someone or something is challenging your relationship. If you are in an established couple, this could mean that either you or your mate are preoccupied or distracted. This card can also mean a rival is on the scene; infidelity or dishonesty may be indicated. In new love matches or if you find yourself alone and seeking, preoccupation with work or monetary goals may not be leaving time or resources for a significant bond to form.

The Seven of Wands reversed can represent the pressure of competition, criticism, or leadership. You may feel overwhelmed or resentful if people have placed too many expectations on you. This can be especially damaging for creative folks who may feel unable to create when they are under pressure. Deadlines and the expectations of others are part of adult life, but stop to consider if you have taken on too much responsibility or too many commitments. Be honest about the battles you are fighting and the reasons why you are fighting them. If these things are forwarding your mission, then stay the course. On the other hand, if you feel like you are paddling upstream and have lost sight of your long-term dreams and goals, you may need to re-evaluate.

———◆———

EIGHT OF WANDS

*Keywords: travel, action, transition,
movement, speed, progress, hope*

The Eight of Wands indicates a time for movement, action, adventure, and travel. It's the green light of the tarot deck that tells us to "go, go, go!" This card may be speaking about transitions or new projects or even a trip you'd like to take. Whatever you have been putting off, it's time to stop procrastinating and make it happen! (And dear reader, while we all want this to mean something fun and exciting, take note that this card may also be hinting at that colonoscopy you have been avoiding.)

In a business or financial reading, this card encourages action, transition, and initiative. Don't wait for folks to ask you to step into new roles—if you want something, go for it. If you see the Sun, Wheel of Fortune, or the Star in your reading, there is clear indication that now is a great time to take a risk. In love or relationship readings, this card often urges us to take that first step, ask that person out, or make that commitment. Sometimes the Eight of Wands counsels us to move forward with a breakup or the dissolution of a relationship. If you are looking for a new match or wanting to reconnect with your mate, a trip or adventure could be in the cards.

Now is a good time for a transition, and if you see the Tower in your reading, you don't really have a choice—change is coming, so you might as well get out in front of it. If this card is in reverse, there may be some action or forward motion that is eluding you at this time, such as bureaucratic setbacks that put a project on hold. In cases like this, you may have to let things sort themselves out. Try to be patient or at least focus on the things you can exert influence over while letting go of those elements that are outside your realm of influence.

———◆———

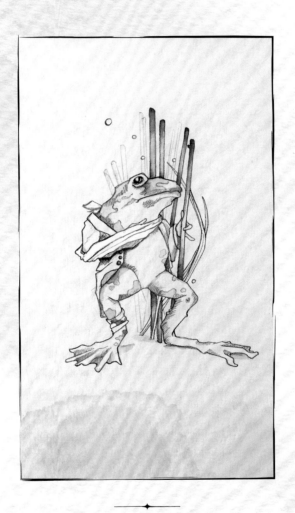

NINE OF WANDS

*Keywords: tenacity, resilience, strength,
perseverance, holding your ground*

The Nine of Wands features an injured and world-weary warrior who holds himself upright with the help of a staff. This character is propped up by the things he has done in life: beliefs, relationships, and accomplishments. No spring chicken, he has a pile of wands behind him that show the many battles fought. This card reminds us that some victories are hard won, and sometimes we just have to stubbornly fight in order to reach our goals.

This card often shows up for a querent when they are struggling with a long-term battle or a challenge that has begun to wear them down. The Nine of Wands represents a marathon rather than a sprint. The message this card holds is about finding inner fortitude and belief in yourself and your ideals. This last leg of the journey is often the hardest. You may be facing some psychological challenges as well as financial or physical. For example, you may be at a point where others have lost faith in you or have voiced doubts about your ability to emerge triumphant. In love or relationship readings, this card can indicate a difficult or challenging road. Perhaps you are caring for a spouse who is ill or have a child or family member with needs that have required sacrifices. Sometimes we see this card in a new love match when one of the parties has a lot of stress or difficulty in their life.

A reversed Nine of Wands can indicate that the querent or someone in their life is creating unnecessary challenges or troubles, like a combative or defiant personality stirring up conflict as one example. Paranoia, defensiveness, and an overly critical outlook can make the world seem like a battlefield. Try to pick your battles wisely and take time to see who your allies are. If you treat those close to you like enemies, you will soon find yourself without any friends.

———◆———

TEN OF WANDS

*Keywords: responsibility, burden, weight,
project completion, milestones, rewards, fatigue*

The Ten of Wands represents the end of a cycle and the weight of responsibility. Unlike the Fool who is at the beginning of their journey, the Ten of Wands depicts the querent at a point in life when they have had some battles, victories, and general life experience. The message of this can be described with a farming analogy: it is not enough to clear the land, sow the seeds, tend and harvest the crops—you also have to carry your produce to market and sell it before the cycle is truly complete. My illustration for this card is of an animal with the fruits of their labors strapped to their back with red string. The red string is a symbol of life and the essential things that connect us to others. Tears spring from the creature's eyes as they push themselves up a cliff and toward an out-of-sight finish line. The intent of the image is to remind us that everything has its burdens as well as its rewards.

In a business, work, or financial reading, we often see this card when a querent is feeling overwhelmed, under tight deadlines, or otherwise pressured. In work or in relationships, heavy responsibilities and commitments may be almost too much for you to carry any longer. This card can manifest when a transition is approaching. Despite the burdens and pressures, this is a positive card because it indicates completion and forward motion.

In reverse the Ten of Wands can indicate needless suffering or remaining in an abusive situation. The micromanagers and perfectionists of the world will see this card with more frequency than the rest of us because they tend to create extra work and stress for themselves.

Learn to delegate; learn to let go of control when it is creating a bad dynamic. If there is a Devil or Temperance card in the spread, there may be a dependency issue weighing on you, e.g., a gambling problem or a codependent relationship. While good things often involve hard work and perseverance, make sure you are working efficiently and that the people and things you are putting effort into are worth your time and life force.

———◆———

PAGE OF WANDS

*Keywords: new ideas, motivation, energy, youth, loyalty,
a message, studiousness, childishness, new erotic adventure*

The Page of Wands indicates creativity, restlessness, and new ideas. You may soon receive a message or meet a new person who inspires you. As the court cards often represent actual people, this page would represent someone energetic, youthful, loyal, and creative. In the past position, this card can speak of your youth or your younger self. In the present or future position, the card most frequently speaks to us of the beginning of a new cycle or project or the arrival of a message or new person.

In a work or professional reading, this card often indicates that you will receive inspiration or a message that will push you in new directions. This could be a promotion, new responsibilities, or information that opens your eyes to opportunities. This card manifests most frequently for creative folks who may suddenly find themselves full of new ideas and motivation. A potential collaborator or project partner may arrive and help take your work in different directions. In general, the Page of Wands represents high energy and a youthful attitude. If you are hoping to meet someone new, there is an erotic element to this card as well: the Page of Wands sometimes indicates the arrival of a new lover or a new phase in an erotic relationship. Relationships with a larger than normal age difference are frequently foretold. In more general relationship, home, or friendship-related readings, this card speaks of the power of creativity and positivity.

Reversed, the Page of Wands cautions against irresponsible or childish behavior. Creative and youthful is great, but nobody likes a flake. The positive energy of the Page of Wands is productive and focused, but when that energy is reversed, it becomes frantic and chaotic. We all have those days where we feel super busy and have a million ideas but end up with nothing to show for all our running around … yeah, those are reversed Page of Wands days. You may need to take some time to be still and re-center yourself. This card can also caution against superficial social or sexual engagements and dangerous or irresponsible sexual behavior. This is especially indicated if the Devil card is present.

———◆———

KNIGHT OF WANDS

*Keywords: action, excitement, acceleration, movement, lust,
travel, generosity, adventure, communication, new ideas*

The Knight of Wands is the most dynamic and action oriented of the horsemen. Like all the court cards, he can represent the querent or someone else in their life; someone energetic, fun, and enthusiastic. This knight is generally pictured on a horse who is galloping or jumping, and in the Otherkin deck they ride a leaping fox. The fox symbolizes the playful intelligence of this card. The knight here has a flower-blossom head, indicating their youthful, spring-like energy and the blossoming of new ideas. Though this person can be very charming, there is an element of impulsiveness and rebellion that should be treated with caution.

In work or financial matters, the Knight of Wands heralds a time of high productivity and new ideas. There is an entrepreneurial spirit present here as this knight is not a rule follower, preferring to jump hedges while others follow the proscribed course. This card can indicate a high-risk and fast work environment; house flipping, start-ups, investment hustles, creative marketing. The Knight of Wands appears in relationship and love readings when there is dynamic or new energy present. This might mean you are about to meet someone new or that your relationship is moving in a new direction. Often the Knight of Wands can be older than the querent but might seem very youthful because of their high energy. Sex and sexual adventure are often indicated by this card, and there may be an...ahem...unconventional aspect to this energy. In the mood for some experimentation? This might be your lucky day. This knight is full of creative power and tends to inspire intense connections, but the flip side is their impulsiveness and inability to follow the rules. The classic Knight of Wands is sexy, fun, creative...and also has terrible credit and possibly a drinking problem.

In reverse the Knight of Wands speaks of frustrations, restlessness, or delays. Hasty decisions can have unfortunate consequences, and impulsiveness may lead to sticky situations. Swords in the reading indicate that your actions have irritated or angered others; a Three or Ten of Swords may speak of relationships ending because of your actions. This card in reverse can sometimes speak of physical injuries or impairments.

———◆———

QUEEN OF WANDS

Keywords: mystery, charisma, warmth,
energy, capability, attraction, power

The Queen of Wands is charismatic, generous, and powerful. She inspires loyalty, dedication, and intense connections. This queen has the creative power of the Queen of Cups but with a darker edge. This queen is intriguing and full of magic. Her intelligence and wit can entertain and attract, but it can also wound. She is at her best as an ally and leader, but her loyalty and support are hard to win. If she represents the querent, they will identify her immediately as their archetype.

If the Queen of Wands is in an influencing position in your reading, it generally indicates that a strong person with a lot of power and charisma has a hand in your future. This is definitely a person that you will want to have working for rather than against you. In work, financial, or professional readings, this card often appears when the querent is in a position of leadership or is forging their way into new ventures. Your intelligence, charisma, and social abilities will serve you well in your current endeavors. The classic indication with this card in a love or relationship reading is that a powerful, charismatic, dark-haired individual will enter your life. As modern tarot readers, we can look a little further than that and see the witch in ourselves and others and channel that magical energy into all aspects of our lives and relationships. This queen has a lot of lessons for us. She teaches us to value our power, to celebrate our bodies, and to wield the magic of attraction. We are sometimes cautioned by this card, reminded of the power and influence we exert over the lives of others. Relationship tensions can arise when friends or partners feel left behind or sidelined by your success and popularity.

The Queen of Wands reversed is a formidable force. All that charisma and power turned away from you can feel like a solar eclipse. If you, dear querent, are this queen (and you know if you are), your power over others can be devastating and must be wielded with compassion. Moodiness and a mercurial nature are the flipside of this queen's creativity and vitality. If things have taken a dark turn, you may need to retreat and engage in some deep self-care before coming back to the world again. If you are dealing with this queen's dark side, here are a few pro tips: give them space and time—being as fabulous as they are is draining, and they may need to recharge. They have a weakness for chocolate, flowers, and the color yellow—send tributes from a safe distance. Lastly, this character more than any other in the tarot deck has a special relationship with cats. If all else fails, place a kitten on them and then hide until they come back to the sunny side of the room.

KING OF WANDS

Keywords: strength, authority, power, fire, warmth,
charisma, charm, manipulation, megalomania

The King of Wands is a powerful card that speaks of charisma, warmth, and authority. This card represents a natural leader with a big picture view and a creative approach to every challenge. In his full power, this king represents an unconventional person who has learned the value of working with others. In their youth this king may have been impulsive and defiant but has since learned how to work within systems. The appearance of the King of Wands in a reading can mean that an opportunity is presenting itself and you have the power and vision needed to take on this challenge.

In a work or finance reading, this card may indicate a time of personal power. Your charisma is high; people will be attracted to you. You have the potential to bring out the best in others and empower them. Fame or high visibility is sometimes indicated. In a love or relationship reading, the King of Wands represents a bold, often showy or theatrical individual who is the focus of attention. Your charisma and personal power magnetically attract others, so be prepared for advances from multiple suitors.

The negative aspect of this card manifests when the King of Wands lets their ego take control. As a natural leader and powerful person, it can be easy to slip into an authoritarian or controlling mode. This card in reverse can mean that the querent has a potentially abusive person in their lives, someone who enjoys having power over others. This king is able to bring out the best in others but is also able to exploit people's weakness when their strength is not balanced with compassion. If you are in a leadership position, be aware of the power you yield. Your goal-oriented vision can blind you to the needs of others if you are not cautious.

———◆———

THE SUIT OF SWORDS
Through air on wings of reason

———◆———

The swords in a tarot deck are associated with the air element. These are cards that speak of the power of the intellect and of the importance of seeing things clearly. The avian representations on the cards urge you to have the sagacity of the owl and the keen eyesight of the hawk. Swords provide counsel when you are in situations where frankness and attention to detail are vital. The court cards in this suit can represent the querent or someone in the querent's life and generally suggest intelligence, wisdom, and good judgment. Swords frequently manifest in readings where we need to set aside feelings and illusions and pay attention to the facts. At their best, the swords are powerful cards that urge us toward clarity and fairness and that teach us to lead calmly and with intelligence. Swords and pentacles are commonly paired as both speak to the material world, money, financial success, and ambition. In their negative aspect, these cards can indicate tensions, controlling behavior, and lack of compassion.

ACE OF SWORDS

Keywords: focus, ambition, power,
mind over matter, confidence, clarity, vision

The Ace of Swords is a strong card that speaks of channeling the power of the intellect into new ventures and situations. There is a clear, cold energy to the Ace of Swords. The emphasis here is on the mind over the heart, and the querent must act with authority and self-confidence. The single upright sword indicates a high degree of focus on one goal. The double edge of the blade is a warning about this kind of single mindedness. Tensions may arise as others might find your behavior cocky or even arrogant, thus the rooster in this illustration. The cold, rocky landscape where the rooster stands alone reminds us of the price of ambition—it can be lonely, uncomfortable, and difficult.

In work, money, and professional readings, this card strongly urges setting very specific goals and to carefully consider the path toward them. There is great power in single minded focus. Insight and mental clarity will be your best assets at this time, so push aside your feelings and focus on the facts. The Ace of Swords often speaks of new ideas and opportunities. In relationship or love readings, your goals may be taking precedence over your relationships. Sometimes this card indicates a break-through or moment of clarity. You may suddenly realize that a relationship or friendship is not helping you be your best self. If you have set aside personal goals or ambitions in order to take care of others, this card may indicate that a time has come for you to reclaim your journey and move toward your dreams. Set goals for yourself and take decisive independent action.

The reversed Ace of Swords can suggest that you have allowed your ambitions to overwhelm everything in your life. This card often pops up for workaholics and for those who let greed or a need for recognition become alienating. Tarot always urges us toward balance. At times, this ace indicates a lack of clarity. You may not have all the facts or information in a particular situation or perhaps have not set clear goals. Specificity and a high degree of focus will aid you on your journey. Lastly, examine your behavior. While this card calls for confidence and standing out from the crowd, you must be aware of the effect your behavior has on others. You can be kind and confident, bold and considerate. Sing your own praises when you need to let folks know that you are available and qualified for a challenge, but remember that nobody likes a braggart.

———◆———

TWO OF SWORDS

Keywords: willful blindness, indecision, denial,
self-deception, stalemate, avoidance

The Two of Swords is a card that in RWS-influenced systems shows a woman wearing a blindfold with two swords crossed in front of her heart. For the Otherkin Tarot, I chose to illustrate this card with the classic trope of an ostrich with whose head is buried in the sand. The offered analogy is of a person who has the truth available to them but is unwilling or unable to face it. Perhaps we do not wish to face the facts as they may seem like too much for us to bear. Perhaps we are choosing to overlook some things because acknowledging them will require us to act, thereby possibly upsetting our lives. In some cases, we may allow others to distort the truth.

This card can indicate a reluctance to face difficult facts. In money matters, you may find yourself struggling with debt, unexpected expenses, or a lack of budgeting that is adversely affecting your situation. In love and relationship readings, this card often shows up for folks who are unable or unwilling to honestly deal with a personal situation. Perhaps you suspect a love interest of infidelity, or maybe you know that your spouse or family member is struggling with something. This card asks that you set aside your feelings and analyze the situation to decide based on facts. You cannot ignore your problems away.

In reverse the Two of Swords can indicate feeling stuck or unable to cope. This card often appears when people are suffering from depression or are overwhelmed by grief, impotence, or feel that they cannot see clearly enough to make a good decision. Sometimes we just have to tear the bandage off, pick a side, and deal with the consequences. The Two of Swords may present a warning to a querent who is deliberately being kept in the dark. If you suspect that you are being manipulated, try to step away from the situation and coldly analyze the actions and motivations of those around you. Trust your intuition and then employ your reason. Some situations may require a clean break.

THREE OF SWORDS

Keywords: wounds, heartbreak, loss,
separation, confusion, past injury, grief

The Three of Swords often appears at times of heartbreak, loss, or betrayal. This card can signify the slings and arrows of life that may have begun to wear you down. However, it can also speak to a large wound, betrayal, loss, or revelation that has you reeling in pain or shock.

In practical matters such as work or finances, this card can speak of injuries or failures that may be undermining your confidence. Has a partner flaked on you? Did an investment not work out? Did you apply for something and were turned down? This card urges us to deal with these difficult things, learn from them and then move forward. Failure is part of life and an essential component of success. In love, friendship, and relationship readings, seeing this card is difficult. In the present or future positions, the indication is betrayal, loss, and grief. This may mean that you are in pain or will soon be injured by the loss of someone close to you or by a difficult revelation such as infidelity or dishonesty. It can also appear when the querent is the one hurting others. If your actions are causing pain to those who love you, consider this a wake-up call. If you are asking about someone's unwillingness to commit, withholding behavior, or lack of motivation, look to their personal history and to past grievances that may be affecting their ability to love and trust.

In reverse this card warns us against self-pity and stagnation. It may mean you are wallowing in past pain or refusing to deal with an injury or physical issue such as depression or addiction. Clinging to failures, heartbreak, or betrayal may have your journey at a standstill. Find new strength and move forward. If you see wands in your reading, the time has come to act. You may have to reconcile with people you have injured or let go of the past.

———————◆———————

FOUR OF SWORDS

Keywords: rest, reflection, planning, convalescence,
recovery, solitude, self-care, balance

The tarot always urges us toward balance, and the Four of Swords reminds us of the importance of rest, reflection, and self-care. In order for you to be at your best and most efficient, you must sometimes set down your swords and care for your mind and body. The illustration for this card is of an owl resting in his nest, but when the night comes, this sharp-eyed hunter will be ready to take flight and find its prey. In the future position the message is encouraging: whatever you are going through now will soon be over, and a time of respite will arrive.

This card often indicates a cessation of activity. Now is a time to watch and listen, rather than act. If you are considering a new direction in your career or branching out into your own business, take a bit of time to make sure your plans are in place. In love and relationship readings, this card most often indicates the need for a pause. If you are thinking about a major change—divorce or career moves, for example—this card suggests taking some time alone to rest and reconnect with your inner self. Humans long for companionship and belonging, but our own voice can get lost when we become overly involved with others. You may be feeling taxed by a difficult relationship or by a friendship in which someone else has current needs or difficulties that have eclipsed your own.

In reverse the Four of Swords can indicate an expenditure of energy that is not contributing to your future success or wellbeing. If you are feeling manic, overwhelmed, or disorganized, it might be time for a total pause. Stress can throw us into disarray. Reclarifying our goals and objectives can enable us to make real progress. In contrast, this card in reverse can speak to the person who has entered a period of delayed progress because of laziness, fear, or depression. If you have felt unable or unwilling to act for a period of time, this card may be calling you out. What are you doing to be your best self? Why are you in a state of stagnation? Make your bed, talk to someone, read a new book, go for a walk. Take care of your body and mind but also keep moving, keep learning, keep fighting.

———◆———

FIVE OF SWORDS

Keywords: conflict, tension, disagreements,
inflexibility, compromise, isolation, defeat

The Five of Swords is a complex card that indicates tension, conflict, and interpersonal difficulties. The image on the card is of a rooster standing at the top of a hill. His position is triumphant but lonely, and the "enemies" are not far away. Sometimes this card indicates a feeling of hollow victory. Perhaps you have won an argument or conflict, but the battle may have cost you more than you realize. Often this card appears when there is danger of alienating friends, lovers, or co-workers through inflexibility or the desire to "be right." At times this card may represent feelings of defeat or the idea that others have turned against you.

This card indicates conflict. All may not be right with your team dynamics or there may be disagreements about which way a project or endeavor should go. If you are in a position of leadership, there may be forces working against you or undermining your authority from the shadows. In relationship readings, this card most frequently appears when there are tensions, disagreements, or petty bickering. There may be stress in a relationship because of finances or things said in anger that are now festering. You may think that everything is fine but there is resentment growing because of an inequality in the relationship or an unhealed wound.

In reverse this card may appear when you are ready for a fight or battle to be over. Perhaps you have come to the realization that fighting is costing you too much and that it is time for you to move on with your life. Forgive and forget, or at least set things aside and focus on what's next. At times this card indicates a conflict that you would like to leave behind but just keeps following you. When this card manifests in the past position, it hints at old wounds or resentments that need to be remedied before you can move on.

———◆———

SIX OF SWORDS

Keywords: movement, travel, escape,
change, new horizons, troubles, challenges

The Six of Swords is a card that often appears at times of transition. It is especially relevant when the querent is contemplating a move away from a problematic or destructive environment, job, or person. Important choices that will affect the course of your life must soon be made. Change can be difficult but there is cause for optimism. Observe that the characters on this card are sailing away from a shore, the embodiment of this card's transitional nature. Look to the place left behind and you will see a building engulfed in flame. While change is always challenging, life sometimes requires radical action for the preservation of the self and the possibility of growth and happiness.

This card often indicates parting ways with an employer, position, or partner. If you have been contemplating a transition, the time may have arrived for you to begin working toward the new future you see for yourself. Unfortunately, in a relationship reading this card does often signify the end of a partnership or friendship. Are you growing, making progress, and moving toward your best self in this relationship? Do you feel safe, cared for, and respected? Are you able and willing to give your best to the person you are involved with? These are answers that should already be quite clear to you. If the answers are no, it might be time to move on. There are occasions when this card speaks to an internal, rather than external, transition. The time may have arrived for you to let go of old wounds, relationships, betrayals, or anything that's preventing you from fully engaging with the present.

The reversed Six of Swords can indicate a refusal or inability to change even when you know it is necessary. We may be held back by fear, laziness, or some external constraint that is preventing desired changes such as debt or a codependent relationship. This card in this position can also speak to an opposite issue: those who never stick to anything. Change can be positive, but nothing can be accomplished without focus. One last note about this card: sometimes this card paired with the Six of Cups in reverse can indicate that someone is contemplating leaving you, breaking away from a partnership, or even actively pursuing other people or opportunities. Trust your gut: if your intuition is telling you that all is not as it seems, prepare for the worst.

————◆————

SEVEN OF SWORDS

Keywords: dishonesty, quarreling, duplicity,
secrets, hidden motivations, sneakiness

The Seven of Swords implies sneakiness and dishonesty. This card speaks to hidden motivations, secrets, and duplicitous behavior. In the illustration, a character slinks away from a camp carrying several swords and a parcel of some sort. There is some anxiety in his expression as he looks back at the folks he has left behind. A black cloud surrounds him and he is now alone, isolated either by his actions or because he has set himself apart. This card most frequently manifests when the querent or someone in the querent's life is keeping secrets or hiding something.

In a work, professional, or financial reading, the Seven of Swords can indicate that the querent is trying to get away with something or is in some way being dishonest. There are situations in which holding back information can spare feelings or protect others or even give us a needed advantage, but secrets can be divisive. At times this card can indicate that someone is working against you, speaking ill of you behind your back, or cheating you in some way. In a relationship reading, this card may point to dishonesty or infidelity. If you have a gut feeling that the person you are involved with is being disingenuous in some way, listen to your instincts. In short, secrets and lies isolate us from each other and diminish our personal power. You may think you are getting away with something, but the indication is to stop to consider the toll that deception takes.

In reverse the Seven of Swords can indicate a feeling of power-lessness, confusion, or the inability to break away from something. Perhaps you know deep down that a friendship or relationship is dishonest or damaging but you feel incapable of ending it. There is a message here about breaking with the past and letting go of baggage that is holding you back.

———◆———

EIGHT OF SWORDS

Keywords: restrictions, self-deception,
denial, negative thinking, isolation

The Eight of Swords shows a blindfolded bird with his foot stuck in a net. He cries out, agonized and panicked, though the net is barely touching his foot and the blindfold is only loosely covering his eyes. This card's message is of feeling trapped, limited, and unable to see a way out. You may be refusing to see how your actions are creating or exacerbating problematic situations. It is likely that you have the information you need to resolve an issue but are refusing to open your eyes and face the facts. There might be an issue in your life that requires brutal honesty and hard work on your part—are you waiting for an easier answer or a quick fix?

In work, financial, and business readings, the Eight of Swords can indicate problems that are causing limitations or are impeding your growth. There *is* a way forward, no matter how dire the circumstances seem. The swords cards call for brutal honesty with ourselves and others. What's required is clear vision and a willingness to set aside emotion in favor of the intellect. The Eight of Swords appears when the querent feels powerless or trapped. If a friendship, partnership, or a situation you are in is making you feel like you have no power over your life, you need to honestly assess the facts and acknowledge that you do have choices, even if those choices are difficult. This card can manifest when there is confusion or a lack of information. There may be people in your life hiding or withholding facts from you, which has made it difficult to see your way forward.

Reversed, this card can indicate that someone is actively manipulating or deceiving you. You may be allowing negative or controlling people to have power in your life. Sometimes this card speaks specifically to denial. If you are in denial about a financial or health issue, be careful: refusing to deal with something generally makes it worse. This card often shows up in abusive personal or work relationships or when the querent is feeling hopeless or overwhelmed. You may feel like there is nothing you can do to improve your situation, but this is never true—there is always hope, there is always a way forward. Pay special attention to health issues when you see this card, as the indication can be that something you are ignoring is going to become problematic.

——————◆——————

NINE OF SWORDS

Keywords: insomnia, anxiety, sleeplessness,
depression, worry, self-torment, despair

The Nine of Swords speaks of anxiety, worry, restlessness, and troubles of a psychological nature. Sometimes these troubles are related to things in your life—finances, relationships, work worries. However, this card addresses not the issues themselves but the ways in which you are allowing negative thinking, self-doubt, and worry to control your life. Sometimes this card indicates worry about the future and approaching changes. We all know that anxiety solves nothing; instead of worrying, this card challenges you to focus your intellect and power on real solutions and actions. Look at the facts: what is the root of the anxiety? Do you feel unprepared for an upcoming challenge? Are there ongoing changes that are causing anxiety? Are you in a position where the only way forward requires a difficult decision, change, or confrontation? The time has come for you to put on your armor and do the hard work. Figure out how to move on with your journey.

In work, financial, and professional readings, this card can indicate concern about your standing within an organization, worries over particular projects, or straightforward anxiety about your finances. Anxiety, frustration, and self-doubt are certainly a part of life, but this card asks us not to allow ourselves to be immobilized by these negative emotions. When the Nine of Swords appears in a love or relationship reading, it often speaks of concerns that we have either about a significant other or about a specific relationship. If a Devil card is also in your reading, it can indicate an unhealthy bond such

206

as dependency or codependency. You may be involved with someone who has debt, health problems, or a substance issue that is affecting their ability to be a good partner. There may be anxiety, worry, or jealousy issues when you feel information is being withheld or when information just doesn't add up. Remember that you have power over your own life—not other people's. Trying to control someone else's journey can derail your own. Focus on the positive, work on yourself, and know when you have to step away from something that is causing you pain or holding you back.

In reverse this card can indicate that you are stuck in a negative headspace and need help to break free. If you have become overwhelmed by doubt, negativity, or depression, you may need to take dramatic steps to get back on course. This card can also indicate that a time of restlessness or anxiety has come to an end. You may receive a message or windfall that will alleviate your circumstances. If you are feeling stuck or overwhelmed, look at the other cards in your reading as they may indicate a place or person where help and support can be found.

———————◆———————

TEN OF SWORDS

Keywords: betrayal, hardship, loss, pain,
disappointment, financial difficulty

In tarot the tens generally represent the end of a cycle, and the Ten of Swords is no exception. If this card is in the past position in your reading, it can indicate that the worst is over, but it can also signify a querent holding on to past pain or betrayal. In the present or future position in your reading, this is a difficult card that heralds heartbreak, injury, or a coming betrayal. If the Tower also appears in your reading, you should prepare for big changes or a revelation that will make you question the foundations of your life and beliefs. Heartache is part of every journey, but even knowing that doesn't make it easier. Accept the pain and think about ways to turn hardship into victory. Remember that every dark night is followed by dawn.

In work, business, or financial readings, the Ten of Swords can indicate loss, betrayal, or failure. The end of a cycle may arrive when you lose a job or a partnership. There may be a time of financial hardship you must pass through. No matter what the circumstance, you must draw deep on your inner strength and fight to maintain a positive outlook. There is always hope and failure is a facet of success—try again, fail again, try better. The manuscript for the first Harry Potter book was rejected by twelve major publishers before becoming one of the most successful books in history; likewise, the Dr. Seuss books saw years of rejection before becoming the international success they would later be. There are countless examples of great success following heartbreaking rejection or failure. Whatever difficulty you are facing, remember that any challenge can be a gateway to positive change.

Perseverance, tenacity, and positivity are your most powerful tools. In love or relationship readings, this card almost always indicates heartbreak. Perhaps the end of a relationship, friendship, or marriage is approaching. In the past position, this card can signify past betrayals or losses that are still having an effect on your or someone else's ability to be a good partner or mate. If there are other swords in your reading, deception may be an issue. You are being asked to take a hard, clear look at what is actually going on.

While the Ten of Swords is never a happy card, it can be even more dire in reverse. The approaching end of a cycle may be very difficult and painful. Most often this card in reverse predicts a situation in which there is nothing you can do (a death, for example) that seals off future possibilities. There are times when the only way forward is acceptance. Some circumstances require tenacity and insistence, but the things outside our power require grace and the willingness to accept the slings and arrows of life. Focus on mending. Rest, meditate on the circumstances, and find the lessons in them. It is not obstacles that define us but how we react to them. Rise, dear querent; no matter the heartbreak, your journey is your own. Make it glorious.

———◆———

PAGE OF SWORDS

Keywords: ability, youth, diplomacy, tact,
intelligence, a message or messenger

The Page of Swords is a delightful card that brings a fresh outlook and new information to your situation. You may soon receive a message or messenger bringing good tidings or a new challenge that can reinvigorate your life. While the pages are often about creativity and new projects, this page is less interested in intuition and feelings and more invested in focus, goals, and ideas. He would describe himself as thinking rather than feeling. The four pages represent youthful energy but may also hint at a certain naiveté. Idealism can be a wonderful force in the world, but it must be paired with action and commitment or you risk becoming a cliché.

In a work or financial reading, this card is a wonderful scion. When you are entering a new project or phase of life the Page of Swords urges you to rely on cleverness, language skills, and observational acumen. This is a card that hails the power of words and ideas. Like any court card, this page may represent someone other than the querent. You may have a new co-worker, contributor, or person of significance enter your professional life. Don't be put off by their keenness or youthful energy; they may have important things to contribute to an ongoing project. In love, friendship, or relationship readings, this often means that a young or youthful person has entered or will be entering your life. This page is strongly related to messages and messengers, be on the lookout for some kind of missive that will impact your life and put a spring in your step.

In reverse the Page of Swords can warn us of careless, blunt words and impetuous behavior. My illustration for this card represents some of the whimsy and fun this card implies. With an envelope in one hand, a jaunty character stands on a hilltop bringing news and energy to the world. The sword in their hand represents the sometimes-careless nature of youth and the wounding ability the truth can hold. Remember to be tactful when you are bringing new ideas or energy to a situation. The Page of Swords can also caution against a manipulative person that may soon enter your life or someone already having an effect on your journey; an adolescent child who can be delightful but also anxiety-producing; a young suitor you are not sure you can trust; an enthusiastic co-worker who steals other people's ideas … these are the kinds of folks represented by this card in reverse. The Page of Swords is a messenger, but do keep in mind that this page may bring unpleasant news in reverse.

———◆———

KNIGHT OF SWORDS

Keywords: strength, intelligence, keenness,
lack of compassion, judgment, conflict

The Knight of Swords, oh boy! This is the most intelligent and perhaps harshest of the horseman. He has vision, strength, and an intellectual approach to the world. Full of new energy and the ability to lead, this card can be a fantastic omen for folks heading into difficult situations or leadership roles. This knight urges you to not let emotion cloud your vision. Keep your goals in clear sight and drive relentlessly toward victory. That said, you risk alienating everyone if you operate entirely without compassion toward others. Focus on facts, numbers, and your aspirations, but try to not run roughshod over the hearts and ideas of others. Apt for this knight, he rides a raptor steed. The energy here is of the hawk or falcon who keenly surveys the land and sweeps in from above to snatch their prey. Merciless, focused, intelligent—this is the Knight of Swords. Remember that the tarot always urges balance, so don't forget to take care of yourself and others on your path to world domination or it will be a mighty lonely throne on which you sit.

In work, professional, and financial matters, the Knight of Swords represents the qualities of loyalty, focus, and integrity. Sometimes you have to be the detail-oriented person who calls out the mistakes of others or the voice of reason that anchors an overly idealistic team. You must be careful with your tone and delivery when pointing out mistakes or sharing opinions with others. Focus on facts, execution (of ideas, not co-workers), and the details.

So you've fallen in love with a Knight of Swords. I offer my condolences. Just kidding (sort of!)—this knight is almost irresistible, so it's understandable. They enter your life with pure energy and vision; the Knight of Swords is the kind of person who knows what they want and is on their way toward it. Their clarity of purpose is swoon worthy, but keep in mind that you will always be playing second fiddle to their ambitions (…until they take an arrow to the knee and give up adventuring, that is). This knight can be a great match for a motivated person who wants to be partnered with an equal. If you are a knight or king or queen yourself, this may be a great relationship for you. Just be careful with your feelings, as the Knight of Swords can be blunt and critical. If this card represents you, dear querent, you probably already know what you're about—you're motivated, focused, intelligent…sound familiar? Try instead to think not just about what you want but also *why* you want it. What is a good life? What is success? If your ambition is not balanced by humanity and compassion, you may find yourself alone and unhappy even after conquering every challenge set before you.

In reverse the Knight of Swords cautions against overly critical, domineering, or controlling behavior. Pursuing goals is admirable but must be balanced by other things. If you are being hypercritical toward yourself or others, you may need to reassess your approach to the world and find ways to reconnect with the compassion, creativity, and nurturing qualities of the cups cards.

——————◆——————

QUEEN OF SWORDS

Keywords: fairness, good judgment,
intelligence, independence, insight, reliability

The Queen of Swords is intelligent, analytical, and trustworthy. Her mind is not clouded by emotion or sentimentality, and she has none of the volatility of the other queens. Yes, she is stern and can be critical, judgmental, and harsh, but if she is on your side, you will have no better ally. She is a natural leader and the kind of person you would want in your crew during a zombie apocalypse. Here is the person who can find the exit while everyone else is panicking. In short, this is a very positive card that speaks of self-mastery and a deep intelligence. She struggles with compassion and can be very critical of others, but it's hard to suffer fools when you are as smart as this lady! This card can represent the querent or someone in the querent's life.

In work and professional readings, you may see this card appear when your keen intellect and critical abilities are most in demand. Bring your intelligence, no-nonsense attitude, and brutal honesty to a situation, as these are the qualities that are most required and will eventually be most valued by others. This card can indicate the possibility of a powerful mentor or ally. There may be someone in your professional life that is formidable and intelligent, yet fair, and they may be a great asset to you. In relationship, friendship, or love readings, this card can indicate that one partner is being emotionally unavailable, aloof, or disconnected. This may represent you or another person in your life, but the message is the same—without compassion and openness to others, our intelligence and competence can become a prison. Critical faculties can be a great asset in your working life, but personal relationships often require a softer approach. Allow yourself a bit of silliness and downtime. If you are in a friendship or relationship with one of these type-A go-getters, learn how to help them unwind. That might mean taking up competitive moose wrestling or whitewater astronomy (I didn't say it would be easy!). Find ways to help them refocus that formidable mind and shut off the critical voice for a little while. This queen is one of the best friends and allies you will ever have, but expect to get cut once in a while.

In reverse this card may indicate that your analytical mind and critical faculties are hindering rather than helping. You may be harming yourself or others with negative thoughts or doubts. Remember, even if you are the smartest person in the room, if your attitude toward others is arrogant or belittling, they won't respect or value your opinions. Never assume that you are the only person who has experienced something. Always approach others with a modicum of humility and compassion for where they are standing. Your intelligence does not guarantee acceptance. This card can indicate that you have allowed a domineering person in your life to take the reins. This person will be intelligent and critical; she may make you wonder about your worth. If someone is making you unhappy or is causing you to doubt yourself, step away from them. Your happiness is your responsibility—never give that power away.

———◆———

KING OF SWORDS

Keywords: authority, maturity, confidence,
wisdom, integrity, judgment, discernment

The King of Swords is a righteous and lawful ruler. He has a strong sense of right and wrong and values fairness and balance. He has many strong qualities and is a natural leader who is respected and valued by others. He does not have the charisma or volatility of the King of Cups or the King of Wands and therefore inspires less fervor but also has fewer enemies. This king is diplomatic and decisive. He sets aside emotion and focuses on facts, and in a reading this tarot card urges you to use these qualities when navigating difficult situations.

In work, professional, and financial readings, the King of Swords is a card that speaks to the value of data, clarity, intelligence, and fairness. This card often appears in a reading for folks who are stepping into leadership roles. When you are fair and thorough, quietly holding your impressive knowledge about your subject, your authority in a group will come from competence rather than charisma. As with any of the court cards, this king can represent the querent or powerful figure in their lives. In relationship, friendship, or love readings, the King of Swords can often represent an older individual in the querent's life, someone stable and respected with good judgment and a cool head. This card can also suggest that the querent channel these qualities in their dealings with others—employ objectivity, equanimity, fairness, and focus on the facts. The illustration on this card is a pelican who has long been a folkloric symbol of dedicated parenthood. If this card represents your mate, they can likely be relied upon to be a stalwart partner and stable element. The cautionary element with this card is about the overly critical tendencies that this king exhibits. He values the intellect over emotion to such a degree that those around him often feel the sting of keen criticism and sharp words. If this card represents you, remember to temper your intelligence with compassion.

In reverse the King of Swords cautions against allowing your intellect to run roughshod over your relationships. Your critical tendencies and intelligence are great assets but can also damage relationships when they are not balanced by kindness and diplomacy. This card may represent someone in your life, a strong intelligent figure who may be hypercritical and domineering. If you have that presence in your life, consider distancing yourself from them, especially if you are internalizing their negativity and judgmental attitude. Pay special attention to this card when there is a Chariot or Hermit in your reading; you may find yourself alone in life if you can't learn how to treat others with respect and compassion.

———◆———

THE SUIT OF PENTACLES
From earth and gold

◆

The pentacles are related to the element earth and speak of material wealth, career, and aspects of your life that dwell in the physical realm—your body, for example, or the home you live in. These cards tend to come up in a reading when money matters are affecting other realms of your journey or when you are pondering financial decisions. In a reading with aces or other movement cards, the suggestion may be that a course of action you are pondering will have financial consequences or rewards. The cards may warn against bad investments, hasty contracts, or unscrupulous partners. Study, apprenticeship, long-term investments—these are areas the pentacles speak to. In relationship readings, pentacles often encourage us to establish strong partnerships such as marriages between equals, and they speak to building family and legacy. There is a conservative element and attitude of prudence present in this suit. They may suggest actions that do not provide immediate gratification but will aid long-term success and overall well-being. Whether you are thinking of having children or are planning for their futures, the pentacles offer substantial guidance. In their negative aspects, the pentacles often speak of greed, materialism, unwise investments, or plans that will not contribute to a solid, prosperous future.

ACE OF PENTACLES

*Keywords: opportunity, favorable financial conditions,
ideas, new partners, inspiration, fertility*

This is a great card to see when you are contemplating a new direction, business, or relationship. The Ace of Pentacles is representative of beginnings that can apply to work, relationships, or even pregnancy. The pentacles correspond to the element of earth and symbolize money and financial concerns as well as the material world and things associated with matter and the body. Pentacles are not idea cards; rather, they deal with actions in the real world. While the wands are about speed and movement, the pentacles require planning, deliberation, and hard work. Of all the aces, this one is the most grounded. I chose a fox for this illustration, but note that it is not the jumping, energetic fox of other cards—this one has all four paws on the ground and an intelligent, alert gaze. All the aces represent new growth and that burst of energy we have at the start of a race, but the Ace of Pentacles in particular is a marathon runner rather than a sprinter. Enthusiasm is great, but it must be coupled with hard work if you want long-term success and prosperity.

This card frequently shows up in work and finance readings as it indicates investments, partnerships, education, and the kinds of activities we do to secure a better future for ourselves and our families. The Ace of Pentacles is a positive card that urges you toward a course of action that will result in prosperity and abundance. When there is more than one ace in a reading, a very strong message is present. In love, friendship, and relationship readings, this card heralds new energy and new connections. If you are actively dating, the Ace of

Pentacles can suggest you should try something new: consider engaging in an activity outside your comfort zone or go out with someone of a completely different type than what you usually look for. In established partnerships, introducing a new element may reinvigorate and strengthen your bond. As a practical card, this ace addresses the body, home, and finances. Take time to think about the ways in which those aspects of your life are affecting your relationship. For example, you may consider cohabitation, having children, or starting a business together.

When the Ace of Pentacles is reversed, be wary of new opportunities and people promising quick returns. Take time to investigate any contracts, business deals, or major purchases. Something that looks like a good idea now may not offer long-term success. When a reversed Ace of Pentacles is in the past position, a failed business, debt, or poor management may be affecting your ability to secure the future you want. For example, impulsive spending in your early twenties may have wrecked your credit or failing classes in college is now preventing you from entering the grad school of your dreams. This card can often represent greedy people or those looking to take financial advantage of others.

TWO OF PENTACLES

*Keywords: balance, multi-tasking, adaptability,
prioritization, time management, flexibility*

The Two of Pentacles is a card that addresses balance, flexibility, and the management of the various parts of our lives that require time and attention. Perched on a branch and holding a balancing pole, a little lemur represents this card in the Otherkin deck. Our lives are full of various forces, of people and projects that push and pull us in different directions. A successful life is one in which we budget our resources well and take care of our mind, body, and community. While often the message is that you are handling things well, the Two of Pentacles can also show up when we need a little guidance with management and allocation of resources.

In work and finance readings, this card can indicate that your time and attention is being split by two or more things. Perhaps you have a busy day job and also a growing side hustle. Maybe you are going to school for one thing while actively working in a different field. This card preaches the gospel of flexibility and balance. Understand your goals and have a pivot plan in case things go awry. In relationship, friendship, and love readings, this card reminds us of the importance of the work-life balance. It's easy to get so caught up in our goals and ambitions that we allow our home life or relationships to suffer. Like anything, a strong relationship requires work and investment and will languish without attention. Embrace the power of saying no, be cognizant of your limitations, and tackle one or two projects at a time instead of ten. Remember that divided we cannot stand, something that applies to you as an individual as much as it does to a society.

In reverse the Two of Pentacles can indicate that you are being pulled in too many directions or that some aspect of your life is creating an unbalanced situation. While balance is an ongoing project for all of us, this card in reverse is a wake-up call—something has reached a tipping point and is damaging you, your relationships, or your future happiness. For example, has work, stress, and long hours led to obesity or a disconnection with your physical self? Has your work, school, or creative life taken so much energy that your primary relationships have withered? Are you spending so much time on recreation, socializing, or drinking that you are not keeping up with work and are earning an undependable reputation? It's time to refocus. You need to take a long hard look at your goals and priorities. Cut the things that are not contributing to your journey, and re-focus your energy on those that are.

◆

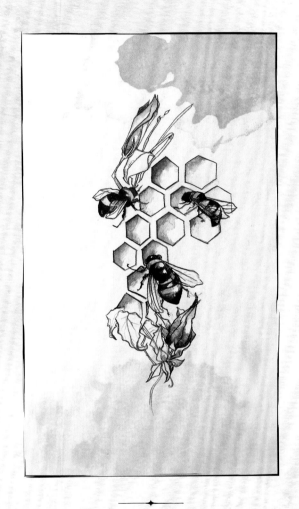

THREE OF PENTACLES

Keywords: diligence, teamwork, apprenticeship,
future building, work, team dynamics

The Three of Pentacles represents the work we do to move toward a specific goal. It speaks of team dynamics, working with others, and good planning. Cards in the suit of pentacles are grounded in practical and financial matters, and this is no exception. Rather than addressing the ideas or abstract goals of a project, this card is about the day-to-day process of creating something; the boots on the ground work it takes to achieve our goals. Honeybees have always been a symbol of hard work, diligence, and teamwork. Alone, there is very little that one bee can accomplish, but as a team a hive can produce twenty to sixty pounds of honey in one calendar year! At times this card reminds us of the limitations of working alone—it may be nudging you toward collaborations or it may speak of specific, existing team dynamics.

This card in a work or financial reading reminds us of the importance of each member of a team. Whether you are the team leader or the most junior member, you are or can become absolutely vital to the work being done. Become indispensable to others by identifying areas that need extra effort. This card is particularly relevant to creative and business ventures, even if you are a solo entrepreneur or someone whose work is primarily as a single independent contractor—stop and consider the ways in which working with others might grow and improve your process. In relationship readings, this card speaks of teamwork and good interpersonal dynamics. Now may be a good time to work with friends on a particular project or collaboration. In love relationships, this card encourages us to see a romantic relation-ship as an opportunity for growth and achievement. The Three of Pentacles is a card representing the possibility of success and the ways in which collaboration and teamwork can help us achieve our dreams.

In reverse this card cautions us against being too insular, guarded, or mistaking pigheadedness for independence. We all need others and should be open to feedback, assistance, and collaboration. This card reversed can indicate negative team dynamics, stress, and inter-personal conflicts.

———————◆———————

FOUR OF PENTACLES

Keywords: prosperity, security, saving,
greed, wealth, materialism, superficiality

The Four of Pentacles in the Otherkin tarot shows an ape grasping his treasure with both hands and feet. He is entirely preoccupied with his jewels and coins; the golden ropes of his stash have wound their way around his hands, rendering him immobile. The creature's expression and posture are defensive—he looks wary, even fearful. This card has a double message. It can encourage a querent to save, invest, and protect their resources and also warns against greed and materialism.

In work and financial readings, the Four of Pentacles speaks to the querent of direct financial issues. This card frequently shows up in readings when a querent has experienced poverty or a lack of resources at some time in their life and is moving through the world with a scarcity mindset, the belief that there will never be enough. The tarot urges us to approach the world with openness and enthusiasm, as operating from a place of fear prevents us from seeing and taking advantage of opportunities available to whomever dares pursue them. In love, friendship, or relationship readings, this card can indicate a withholding or guarded demeanor. You may be so preoccupied with protecting yourself that you cannot open your arms and embrace others. In some cases, the card can indicate that the querent or someone in their lives is clinging to negative attitudes that stem from emotional or financial poverty in the past. For example, you may have had a parental figure who was very critical and unable to show affection, which has caused you to now close off parts of yourself and become unavailable to others. The Four of Pentacles is most directly a card about money. In the present position, this card can indicate that this is how others see you: preoccupied with money, greedy, or stingy.

In reverse the Four of Pentacles is a card that speaks of the opportunities for growth and joy that you may be missing. You may be placing so much emphasis on the material and accumulation that your relationships, health, and daily happiness are being adversely affected. Tarot always urges balance, so plan for the future but allow yourself to enjoy each day. Protect yourself and your resources but don't become defensive and paranoid. This card can also appear in a reading when the querent's relationship to money is out of wack. Compulsive shopping, gambling, or financial dishonesty can be indicated. We all long for financial security and prosperity and the tarot can help us achieve our goals but it also reminds us at every turn that relationships, creativity, and health are things we must treat with equal emphasis and investment.

———◆———

FIVE OF PENTACLES

Keywords: hardship, loss, poverty, set backs,
charity, unemployment, injury, health issues

The Five of Pentacles speaks of adversity, setbacks, and personal challenges. You may find yourself struggling to make ends meet or you may have to deal with an injury or illness that is preventing you from living your life as fully as possible. Like the fives in each of the suits, this card represents situations of adversity or conflict. The illustration on this card is of a creature limping along on crutches, they wear a ragged coat and have a tin cup in one hand in which to collect spare change from those passing by. Though a black cloud hangs over them there is also an illuminated church window behind them indicating that an organization or simply the querent's faith may help them at this time. This card often urges us to seek help from others or reach out to someone who needs a helping hand. Compassion and humility are the two messages this card carries. Compassion for others who may be struggling and the humility to ask for help when we are facing overwhelming adversity.

In work, professional, or financial readings, this five can indicate unwelcome losses: lay-offs or a period of unemployment, debt, or financial struggle. You may find yourself demoted at work or an income stream that your budget depended on may suddenly dry up. Look to other cards in the reading for advice about how to get past these hurdles. There are countless ways to be of service to others, and making that effort can sometimes be the first step to turning your own situation around. In a relationship, friendship, or romance reading, the Five of Pentacles can indicate that you or someone close to you is going through something difficult that is preventing them from fully engaging in a partnership or friendship. There may be a health issue, difficult loss, or lack of resources that feels like it is squeezing the joy out of life. Be honest with those around you about what is holding you back, and if someone close to you is suffering, the deck is urging you to help. When this card appears in the past position, it can indicate that a past loss, illness, or poverty is shaping your life and that until you let those things go, you will be unable to move forward with an open heart.

In reverse this card is very situation dependent. On the one hand, it can indicate that a time of hardship is coming to an end. On the other, it can mean that hardship or adversity has not been dealt with or has been internalized and has become resentment, fear, or a belief that the world is out to get you. While we cannot control everything in life or the difficulties that come our way, we do have absolute power over how we react to them. It takes enormous grace to accept loss, injury, and pain, so we want to avoid the other option: blame others, become angry, and turn our pain into poison that will eventually corrode joy in our lives. More than anything, this card urges us to reach out to others for help when we need it and offer help when we can give it.

———◆———

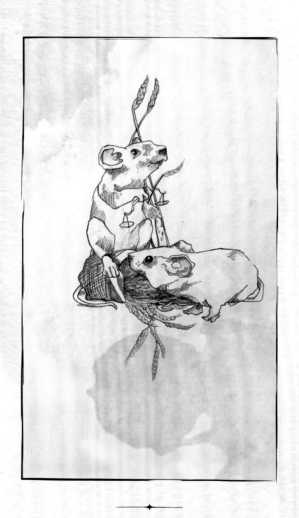

SIX OF PENTACLES

*Keywords: community, generosity, mentorship,
hosting, involvement, helping others*

The Six of Pentacles addresses community and balance. This card represents giving to others, accepting help when we need it, and sharing abundance. Unlike the Five of Pentacles, this is not a charity card or one that indicates a crisis or an acute situation. Rather it speaks to general attitudes and activities within a community. This is a card that can be seen as a positive omen, at times it just lets us know that we have support and people that care about us even if we feel alone. It can also remind us of the importance of playing an active role in the lives of others through mentoring, friendship, or just listening. Sometimes you might be the mouse in the illustration with the big bag of wheat, and at other times you might need to accept support or resources from others. This card guides us toward acceptance with grace and giving with an open heart.

In work and professional readings, the Six of Pentacles urges us to remember that even if we work alone, we are still part of a larger community. When you see this card in a reading, it may be urging you to reach out to peers or mentors, or to put more energy into the public-facing aspect of your work or practice. If you have the ability to help others with advice, mentorship, or resources, now may be a good time to invest energy in that. In love, friendship, and relationship readings, this card can speak to balance within friendships and the ways in which we show up for each other. In the most obvious readings, this card can indicate economic disparity; for example, meeting a wealthy love interest or dating someone with far fewer resources than you. These differences may be causing tension and should be addressed. Whether you are the one giving or taking, remember that relationships thrive when there is balance. If you are willing to take, you must be willing to give; people will soon feel taken advantage of if you don't.

In reverse this card warns of situations where social imbalance is becoming problematic. If you have relied economically on others, there may be growing resentments that will begin to destroy relationships. You may be giving more than you should to someone ungrateful or unworthy. In general, generosity and openness are laudable and good for the soul, but there are people out there who will take until there is nothing left—not just money; it may be time, resources, or your emotional energy. Know a vampire when you have one in your life and protect yourself against them! In more abstract terms, this card can warn us about attitudes or approaches to the world that do not serve our best interest. Greed, pettiness, selfishness—we all have these attributes to varying degrees, but this card warns us when we have allowed those unattractive traits to become guiding principles.

———◆———

SEVEN OF PENTACLES

*Keywords: investment, vision, hard work,
effort, long-term success, failure, perseverance*

The Seven of Pentacles represents the long-term success that results from hard work and perseverance. A garden or gardener accurately describes the message of this card as they illustrate sowing the seeds of future success. Like a gardener, we should be prepared for some failures along the way: not every seed takes root, not every flower survives the harsh and temperamental frosts of spring. We must accept that we will win some battles and lose others, but overall we keep our eyes on our major goals and move toward those things with intent and a sense of purpose.

When seen in a business, creative, or financial reading, this card often indicates that the querent feels frustrated or disillusioned with the work they are doing. Perhaps you felt you would be further along by now; perhaps your daily efforts seem overlooked or ignored as less experienced or less talented people appear to be moving ahead. This card asks you to keep your eyes on the long game—life is a marathon, not a sprint. In love, friendship, or romance readings, this card speaks of deep bonds and long-term partnerships. Every relationship goes through periods of closeness and distance, but shared history is very hard to replace. Now may be the time to reconnect with old friends or previous lovers. You may want to think about marriage, children, or a renewal of vows. If you are dating or seeking love, this card can indicate that a long-term match is in the picture and that you should be prepared for the kind of investment that a substantial relationship requires. If this card is in the past position, it may indicate the loss of a significant other or distance that now exists between you and someone who was a significant part of an earlier phase in your life.

In reverse the Seven of Pentacles urges us to avoid the quick and easy. Be wary of new relationships with charismatic people or those who immediately seem excessively available. It takes time to form real bonds—be open to others but wary of those who offer too much for too little. This card can condemn the querent for lacking focus, diligence, or a solid work ethic. In reverse, this card can indicate that you need to adjust your attitude toward failure. You may feel crushed by things beyond your control and are forgetting that success often follows failure, sometimes years of failure! Rejection, loss, and difficulty are part of life. Not everything we put effort into will yield fruit; not every battle is won. Sow many seeds, work the field. Remember that success is most often the reward of diligence rather than luck.

EIGHT OF PENTACLES

Keywords: craftsmanship, skill, potential, business,
industry, accomplishment, hard work

The Eight of Pentacles is often called the apprenticeship card. It speaks to learning new skills or expanding an existing skill set in a new direction. The message here is about the kind of time, investment, and hard work required to achieve mastery or build a business. The Eight of Pentacles addresses the actions we must take to wrangle those bursts of inspiration into the physical world.

This card applies most directly to professional, educational, or work-related queries. If you are already in an apprenticeship position or are dedicated to training, studying, or mastering a skill, this card may simply offer a message of affirmation, a pat on the back to let you know you are doing the right thing. The slow, upward climb toward training for a profession, vocation, or building a business can be grueling, but rest assured that your efforts will pay off eventually. On the other hand, if you are unhappy with the path you are on or you have discovered that you no longer have a passion for what you are doing, it may be time to pivot or even start over. This card may also be encouraging you to make a radical shift toward apprenticeship. It is very possible that we get one shot at this journey, so don't waste it doing something you don't love! Much like a craft or business, if you don't put the time and effort into your relationships they will not prosper. In friendship and established relationship readings, this card can pop up for a querent who needs to apply diligence and study to their relationships with others. This can mean counseling, therapy, or working on the basics of communication and interpersonal dynamics.

Don't assume that relationships deserve less time or effort than your work—they need tending, and thoughtful effort to thrive. In new love readings, this card can indicate that the querent will meet a student, apprentice, or someone working toward specific goals. This person may be found in a work or school type situation. Perhaps they are an apprentice in your trade or someone who is part of a project you are contributing to. Sometimes this card speaks to changes you might be pondering. If the Hermit is also in your reading, now may be a good time to be alone and to focus your energy on your work rather than on relationships.

In reverse this card may indicate wasted efforts, discouragement, or reaching a plateau or roadblock. You may feel you are wasting time or that the time you have put into something is not yielding fruit. In contrast, this card can also mean that you are expecting results but have been unwilling to do the work. You may see this card if you are operating with entitlement and are surprised when your ideas or projects are not immediately met with success.

————◆————

NINE OF PENTACLES

Keywords: success, abundance, self-esteem,
maturity, discernment, balance, strength

The Nine of Pentacles represents a mature, self-contained, and self-motivated individual. The clear vision and intellectual drive of this card seem almost more at home in the suit of swords. Additionally, the character on this card is generally illustrated with a bird—a hawk, falcon, or other creature of the air, again the associated element of swords. However, her feet are on the ground and the lush gardens in which this archetype lives indicate someone who has harnessed their high ideals, critical thinking, and focus and used those tools to prosper and grow in the earthy and grounded garden of pentacles.

In business and financial readings, this is a powerful card that speaks of prudence with money, long-term investment strategies, and discipline. The economics represented here are those that blend focus and a cool head with the sensual and physical—a winemaker, for example, or hospitality-related businesses such as hotels, spas, or restaurants. This is not a card that represents the beginning of a journey or idea but rather the kind of reward that awaits those who pursue their passion with discipline and drive. When this card is in the future position, it is a great omen of success and offers affirmations to the querent; you are on the right track, work hard and remain focused and a life of abundance will unfold for you! In love, relationship, or friendship readings, the Nine of Pentacles speaks of self-awareness, discipline, and the work we do to become the best individuals, and therefore the best partners, we can be. This card encourages us to focus on developing our own minds, bodies, and skills. When you are the best version of yourself, you will inspire others and bring value to their lives. This nine often represents a person who is quite content with their own company. Despite having friends, family, and loved ones, they are not needy or dependent on the outside world for validation. There is a strength and maturity that comes from doing the work of self-mastery. If there are strong social or romance cards such as the Lovers or Three of Cups in your reading, it points to efforts at self-development bearing fruit in your life; strong partnerships and deep bonds will be your reward.

In reverse the Nine of Wands holds many cautions. Be careful with your hard-won resources. Your generous nature and inclination to help others may open the door to abusive people who don't have your best interests at heart. When you have done the work that results in prosperity, others may try to erode your self-esteem or diminish your accomplishments. This card also strongly admonishes us against martyrdom or neglect of the self in order to serve the interests of others. While there are times in life when caring for a loved one may take precedence over our immediate plans and goals, we must always remember that our lives are our responsibility. If you are unhappy or unfilled, you have less to offer. Focus on self-care and self-development. Another caution: in reverse, this card can warn against an unwise investment. You may be putting time, energy, or money into something that is not as it seems. Protect yourself and your resources; don't overcommit, and if your gut is warning you about someone, listen to your intuition!

◆

TEN OF PENTACLES

*Keywords: long-term partnership, happiness,
stability, prosperity, wealth, family, love*

The Ten of Pentacles is one of the happiest and most stable cards in the deck. It's wonderful to see in the influencing or future positions in a reading as it indicates that deep bonds, stability, and love are available to the querent or will be soon. This is the card of a mature relationship or partnership in which each individual is supporting the other and helping them reach their goals. This is not a light love and romance card; rather, it speaks to the kind of relationship that is built over time with effort and trust. I chose to use different animals in this rendition of the card—a fox and rabbit—because this message is not about codependency in a way that subsumes one person's will or identity to the other. This card celebrates the kind of partnership that lifts both individuals toward self-actualization and their best selves.

In romance, friendship, or even work readings, this card speaks of strong partnerships and urges us toward them. While there are many journeys and adventures we can tackle on our own, collaboration and cooperation can expand our opportunities and ideas exponentially. In fact, I have personally noticed that this card tends to come up in readings where spouses or close friends are creating a successful business together. If you have this kind of partnership already, rejoice and find your strength in it. You already know what a priceless and precious thing it is.

Offspring are always present with the Ten of Pentacles, often represented by children; whether the relationship in question is romantic or platonic, this kind of partnership always yields fruit. This card can present a very encouraging message to a querent; continue to work hard and stay focused because you are building a beautiful future for yourself and your family. This is also a positive omen for those inquiring about a relationship, material acquisition, or the expansion of a family. In difficult times, we are reminded of the friends and family from which we can draw strength and support.

You may be seeing this card as a representation of an already existing relationship in your life, or it may be urging you to connect with a mentor, community, or someone in your industry who shares your goals. If this kind of relationship is your goal and has evaded you thus far, look to the other cards in your reading. If you see other pentacles, you likely need to work on yourself and on personal goals before you will be ready to be a good partner to someone else. The presence of court cards could indicate that your match may be in the picture already.

In reverse the Ten of Pentacles cautions against behaviors that place our relationships at risk. The trust and support of others is hard-won and can be delicate. Once lost, precious partnerships can be broken forever. If you are being duplicitous or engaging in behaviors that jeopardize your future, beware—these things have a way of coming to light. You may be facing a difficult breakup, loss, or betrayal. A relationship you thought was stable and strong has disappeared or become untrustworthy. Something or someone may be attempting to undermine a partnership, so be on guard, especially if you see a conflict card. In a relationship reading, this card reversed cautions that the long-term potential you were hoping for isn't there, or in a marriage it may indicate that the future is not stable or secure.

———◆———

PAGE OF PENTACLES

Keywords: investment, study, future planning,
prosperity, good luck, new ventures, pregnancy

The rabbit illustrated on the Otherkin Page of Pentacles carries a large gold coin, reminding us of the card's connection to wealth and the world of finance. Behind the bunny a tree blossoms with golden fruit, indicating that the planting of seeds will become a future tree; in time, the tree will bear a harvest. Like all the pages, the Page of Pentacles has a youthful energy and is a wonderful omen at the beginning of new ventures. This card encourages us to embark on projects that will build our knowledge, skill set, and financial future. In a reading this page often urges us toward reinvigorating or reinventing our lives in some way. You may be pondering new opportunities, courses of study, your own business, or a new creative partnership. Now is a good time to set clear goals and focus on making them reality. While other cards address the dreaming and scheming part of this process, the Page of Pentacles speaks of implementation of plans and real-world effort. The pages often represent the arrival of a message, messenger, or gift; in this case, the message may be of a financial nature.

In a work, business, or financial reading, this card speaks of new ventures and investment in your future. There is a distinctly practical vibe to this card; the Page of Pentacles urges you to stop dreaming about prosperity and begin taking real action toward it. Whatever the next step is, stop pondering—make specific goals and plans. In love, friendship, and relationship readings, this card often represents a young or youthful person who has entered or will be entering your life. The pages do not represent a specific gender and can be anyone in your life; in this case, they are likely youthful but with a studious demeanor and the willingness to work hard. The Page of Pentacles can also represent conception, pregnancy, and new life. While the other pages speak of new ideas and inspiration this card is about putting in the work; if you see it in a relationship context you may need to think about investing more effort into your relationships. If you want long-term success, you are going to have to do the work. The pages are strongly related to messages and messengers, you may receive news or a missive that has the potential to impact your future.

In reverse the Page of Pentacles can represent flakiness, wasted time, unrealistic ambitions, or laziness. You may see this card if you or someone in your life is always chasing the quick buck or the easy fix instead of really investing in the future with sound strategies and hard work. Be cautious when you see this card reversed in a financial reading, as it can mean that a new opportunity that looks good now will not be successful in the long run.

—————◆—————

KNIGHT OF PENTACLES

*Keywords: responsibility, long-term planning,
maturity, trust worthiness, stagnation*

The spirit animal of a Knight of Pentacles would likely be a tortoise or an elephant, a creature whose energy is stable, stalwart, and intelligent. Sure, this guy is technically a horseman and warrior, but he is neither the romantic and charming Knight of Cups nor the daring, impulsive Knight of Wands. He doesn't look before leaping; this knight doesn't leap at all! He calmly assesses situations and moves slowly and deliberately. Associated with financial stability and long-term planning, this card is a good omen for a querent who would like to bring those elements to their lives. Here we have a knight riding a turtle rather than the plough horse you might be accustomed to seeing in other decks. This visual is a reminder of the nature of the Knight of Pentacles. His personal motto could easily be "slow and steady wins the race."

In a professional or work-related reading, the Knight of Pentacles may indicate stability and a time for investing in long-term plans rather than seeking instant gratification. This is not generally a card that speaks of change, unless it is toward greater stability. Look to adjacent cards and card placement. This knight in an influencing position can indicate an ally, boss, or friend upon whom you can depend. The person may be older or a representative of a more conservative or traditional way of operating. In a romance or relationship context, the Knight of Pentacles can represent an older or more mature love interest. The cards may be suggesting that a stable, conservative partner is a good match for you at this time or indicate that this is the role you are being called to assume. If you see two knights in a reading, a rivalry of some sort could be indicated, especially in conjunction with a conflict card such as the Five of Wands.

In reverse this card can indicate stagnation and a lack of creative or professional drive. Making good long-term decisions is not the same as being so set in your ways that the world begins to leave you behind. The reversed Knight of Pentacles is stable to the point of being boring and so conservative in his decisions that he is no longer relevant. If this card turns up in a personal reading, the deck may be urging you to try new things, shake up your routine, or embrace change. Are you missing out on important opportunities because you have become too stuck in your current way of thinking or acting? This card may also represent someone in your life such as a love interest, family member, or professional contact.

———◆———

QUEEN OF PENTACLES

*Keywords: productivity, fertility, wealth, success,
nurturing, home, happiness, prosperity*

The Queen of Pentacles is a kind and generous spirit. Everything good about motherhood is represented by this card. She is grounded, complex, nurturing, and fully self-developed. Here is the model of leadership that celebrates and brings out the best in others. Strongly related to reproduction and fertility, this card is a wonderful omen for anyone looking to expand and grow. Whether you are trying to scale a business or are thinking about having children, this ultimate earth mother archetype could not be better to see in a reading.

In work, professional, or financial readings, the Queen of Pentacles indicates expansion, growth, and prosperity. She can represent a specific person in your life, a powerful and nurturing mentor, for example, who may have valuable support or counsel to offer. This card can also indicate that a "motherly" leadership style will serve you well at this time. Nurture, encourage, and protect—this is the path to prosperity under this queen. If you see this card alongside others from the suit of pentacles, there is a strong material or financial leaning to your reading. Now may be the time for expansion or for resources to be allocated to growth. In readings regarding friendships, love, or relationships, this queen is a good omen for fertility and growth. It could mean actual conception, pregnancy, or childbirth, or it can also apply to partnerships in which people are trying to build toward mutual goals. At times, this card asks you to step into a caretaker role. You may need to be the one offering support to a loved one or close friend. The nurturing protective energy of this card is so strong and immensely attractive to others, don't be surprised to find yourself in community leadership roles if you are channeling this card! This queen can represent someone in your life, an ally that you can turn to in difficult times, someone compassionate and wise. The card may indicate that it is time for you to step up and embody the qualities of this queen: your generosity, nurturing, and protective instincts may be called upon to help a loved one in a time of trouble or to lead a community. The Queen of Pentacles can sometimes bring a simple message to a querent: focus on your home life and family; you are needed there.

In reverse this card cautions against domineering or controlling behavior. You may see this card if your concern for others has become stifling or oppressive. The job of the mother is *not* to keep their off-spring trapped in the nest but to nurture, protect, and, at some point, push them to test their wings. To truly want the best for others often means letting them go. This card cautions against nagging, domineering behavior that beats down rather than builds up. You may have let caring for others overwhelm your own journey and have lost some of your identity in the process. Remember that this card represents a fully actualized person, not a martyr but a queen—a powerful, mature person who has nurtured herself as well as others. Have you forgotten your own journey? Are *you* still growing and changing? A last word of caution: this card may represent a powerful woman in your life who is working against you or who claims to have your best interest at heart but is actively undermining you and your journey.

KING OF PENTACLES

Keywords: maturity, wisdom, prosperity,
accomplishment, authority, aptitude

The King of Pentacles is the ultimate symbol of material and worldly success, authority, and financial security. He is the tarot deck's patron saint of prosperity; there is almost no better card to see if you are presently working toward a material or financial goal. Here is a symbol of the kind of effort and wise investments that result in stability and prosperity.

The King of Pentacles most clearly presides over business and financial readings, his realm and domain. He can provide affirmation to a querent embarking on a course of study, investment, or a new job. Good things are down the road for you if stay the course. If you are moving into a position of leadership or are expanding your current artistic practice or business, this card counsels you to pay close attention to the numbers: budgets, contracts, pricing structures, and margins are this king's preoccupations. This card indicates a focus on financial success and may represent someone who can help you in that journey—a mature, successful person in your life. In the most obvious of love or relationship readings, this card can indicate a potential or current match with an older, prosperous person. The classic interpretation of this card would be that "you will soon meet a wealthy older man," and that may in fact be the message this reading holds for you. Though this card often represents someone specifically male gendered, tarot is very mutable when it comes to these things, so don't rule out the possible appearance of a strong older woman or person with feminine energy. You may already know this person or be in a relationship with them, or you yourself may be assuming the role of advisor, patron, or provider within a partnership. The message of this card is about the physical and material realm. For example, this card may show up in an influencing position when your mate is willing or able to provide the financial stability required for you to pursue a creative or educational project. Your reading may simply affirm that you have the resources and support you need to explore new paths.

Be cautious with your resources, dear querent, when you see a reversed King of Pentacles—the warning is about unwise investments, gambles that won't pay out, or behavior that is going to hurt long-term stability or prosperity. The flip side of the generosity and prosperity of this king is miserliness and greed. Are you so focused on profit and accumulation that your relationships and spiritual or emotional life are drying up? Is an obsession with future prosperity making your day-to-day life a portrait of deprivation? This card may specifically depict someone in your life who is materialistic, controlling, or greedy. You need to distance yourself from that kind of energy, lest it not only slow your progress but derail your journey in devastating ways. Be cautious of financial deals at this time, read the fine print, verify claims, and don't invest more than you can afford to lose.

———————◆———————

CONCLUSION

The creation of the Otherkin tarot deck was a labor of love, and I hope it comes across with each card. Thank you for allowing my work to be a small part of your journey; may it help you along the way or at least provide some entertainment. I know some of you are probably deck collectors or professional readers, while others may be just beginning their practice or reconnecting after a time—in each case we are communing with a long historical legacy of folks that includes witches, diviners, fortunetellers, healers, and artists. We are a tribe, and I appreciate each one of you.

No matter how you use the tarot, it is a powerful tool that aids in understanding ourselves, the dilemmas we face, and the archetypes we represent. I truly believe that tarot can help us lead more examined lives and am proud to be part of that endeavor. Whether you received this deck as a gift or chose it for yourself, I'm glad that it is now in your hands. I sincerely hope that the Otherkin deck becomes a well-used feature in your practice and that these cards bring you closer to others, provide insight, and offer enjoyment.

Happy reading, dear querent, and may your journey be glorious.

—Siolo

To Write to the Author

If you wish to contact the author or would like more information about this book, please write to the author in care of Llewellyn Worldwide, and we will forward your request. Both the author and publisher appreciate hearing from you and learning of your enjoyment of this book and how it has helped you. Llewellyn Worldwide cannot guarantee that every letter written to the author can be answered, but all will be forwarded. Please write to:

Siolo Thompson
c/o Llewellyn Worldwide
2143 Wooddale Drive
Woodbury, MN 55125-2989

Please enclose a self-addressed stamped envelope for reply, or $1.00 to cover costs. If outside the USA, enclose an international postal reply coupon.